D1477029

ALDERNEY

AT WAR

1939-49

ALDERNEY
AT WAR
1939-49

Brian Bonnard

ALAN SUTTON

First published in the United Kingdom in 1993 by
Alan Sutton Publishing Limited · Phoenix Mill · Far Thrupp · Stroud · Gloucestershire

First published in the United States of America in 1993 by
Alan Sutton Publishing Inc · 83 Washington Street · Dover · NH 03820

British Library Cataloguing in Publication Data

Bonnard, Brian
·Alderney at War
I. Title
942.343084

ISBN 0–7509–0343–0

Library of Congress Cataloging in Publication Data applied for

Typeset in 11/13 Bembo.
Typesetting and origination by
Alan Sutton Publishing Limited.
Printed in Great Britain by
The Bath Press, Bath, Avon.

To all victims of tyranny and oppression everywhere, but especially to the people of Alderney who had to abandon their homes and possessions.

Also to those brought here in slavery, many of whom died in Alderney during the period of Nazi occupation 1940–45, or later, as a result of their imprisonment here.

Contents

Alderney Relieved

STATES OF ALDERNEY

From the President's Office

Alderney Channel Islands

The Second World War was the single most significant event in the history of Alderney. It altered the island both physically with the innumerable fortifications built by the Germans and, more importantly, the comparatively few islanders who returned over the years were changed by their experience in the wider world.

Before the war, Alderney was a peaceful backwater largely dependent on agriculture and the export of granite. The evacuation took virtually the whole population away. Those who returned had experienced the wider world of Britian at war. Many had served in the forces and a number had married people from 'away'. They expected higher material standards consistent with the hopes of a newly elected socialist Government in the UK.

After the war, the island was strewn with remnants of the occupation – guns and ammunition, the grey and blue pyjamas of prisoners, sandals made from car tyres, papers everywhere. I was a small boy then, but even now I remember the silence due to the lack of birds when we came back, the large alsatians who had been trained to bite anyone who ran, and also the dentist who stayed on long after the other Germans had left and who used his treadle drill in Cooley's shop.

Until now, there has been a large gap in our knowledge of what happened in Alderney during the war. There have been many rumours and sensational articles in the newspapers. Now this material has been meticulously sifted in the light of recent revelations. There will no doubt be further revelations, but Brian Bonnard has evaluated all the various sources now available, including the most recent ones from the Public Records Office, with modesty and precision. Nobody can still be certain of the number of people who died in Alderney during the war, but he has given us a rounded picture of life on the island during these last years.

To understand Alderney today it is essential to know the 'unknown' history of the island during the war.

J. KAY-MOUAT

Acknowledgements

The author and publisher are grateful to the following for permission to use photographs and to copy documents:

The Alderney Library Committee, for permission to use photographs from the Herzog collection; the Alderney Society, for permission to use the 9.5 mm cine film, photographs from the Asbeck collection and others, and several of the maps and plans; the Channel Island Occupation Society; the German Occupation Museum, Guernsey, for the photographs of the pigs in Victoria Street and the reconstruction of the interior of a gun emplacement; the Imperial War Museum, for printing the photographs from the 9.5 mm cine film; A.A. McGregor, for several of the 1946 photographs; the States of Alderney, for permission to photograph the document listing graves in the churchyard. The aerial photographs have been enlarged from small portions of several series of RAF reconnaissance photographs in the possession of the Alderney Society, by kind permission of the RAF Museum.

Other contemporary photographs, documents, press cuttings, and recent photographs are from the author's own collection.

Alderney at Peace, spring 1939

In the spring of 1939 the peaceful community of Alderney numbered about 1,500 men, women and children. The island was almost a kingdom on its own, while owing its allegiance directly to the English Crown. The 'ruler' was the judge, Judge F.G. French, elected in 1937, who was responsible for both the civil administration and legal affairs of the island.

In legal matters the Judge was supported by the Procureur, who had a seat on the States but no vote, and the Greffier, who acted as Clerk of the Court. They were both paid. (The 'States of Alderney' was for centuries both the island's Parliament and Court. Since 1949 the two functions have been separated.) The Sheriff, the Sergeant, the Constables and six unpaid Jurats were also elected, the latter from among those ratepayers whose property was valued at more than 20 quarters of wheat rent, by then about £400 p.a. (Wheat was fixed at 4s. 6d. a bushel in 1939.) Together with the Judge, the Procureur and the Greffier these members constituted the Court of Alderney, governing the island with laws going back to Norman times, and the observance of customs and traditions which had existed from 'time out of mind', a phrase usually sufficient to ensure the acceptance of the claim made. Once elected, Jurats served until the age of 70 without being re-elected, and because of the property-value requirement the office tended to remain within a few families. The electors also had to be ratepayers, that is property owners, aged 20 years or over for males and 21 years or over for females, and in this case either single or widowed. Married women were not allowed to vote since under the Norman laws they could not own property. Publicans and Roman Catholics were also barred from voting, and from membership of either the Court or the States. The Court when in session had to consist of the Judge and at least two Jurats.

Legislation was carried out by the drafting of *Projets de Loi* which, when agreed and after being presented to the electors, had then to be approved by the Privy Council, representing the sovereign, and were embodied as 'orders-in-council', which were subsequently 'registered' in both Alderney and Guernsey. The orders-in-council were drafted in both English and French, while all property transactions and bonds brought before the court were written in French only, and signed by two Jurats, after the parties concerned had expressed their verbal agreement to the court. The persons involved did not themselves sign the documents.

The remainder of the administrative body consisted of the *Douzaine*, twelve elected owners of property of lesser value (10 quarters or more of wheat rent). They were elected for a term of three years, with the longest serving four members retiring each year. They could be re-elected until they reached the age of 60. Five of them sat in the States along with three People's Deputies, elected by the ratepayers to represent them on the States. They in turn all sat, with the Judge and Jurats, on the Court of Chief Pleas held twice a year, and requiring the presence of the Judge, and at least seven other members.

As distinct from Jersey and Guernsey where all proceedings were conducted in French, in Alderney either French or English could be used, the local 'parler' having declined greatly with the influx of immigrant workers and troops in Victorian times. The *Billets d'Etats* (the proposed items for discussion at the next sitting of the States), were produced and printed in both languages. They were issued free to all who demanded a copy. The option for members to address the courts or the States in either language often created confusion in those members who were not fluent in the French language, and sometimes created dissension at the sittings.

Before each States' meeting, a People's Meeting was held for the purpose of explaining the contents of the *Billet* to the people, especially those (by that time probably few), who could not read, and answering questions about the various items. At that time this meeting was held simply due to tradition, but after the war the practice was included in the statutory law of the island, making it unique among both the Channel and British Isles.

The *Douzaine* were responsible for regular inspection of the roads, carried out on New Year's Day and quarterly, and for settling any boundary disputes which might arise between relatives or neighbours. They knew the ownership and boundary markers of every piece of land, a difficult task when the Norman laws of inheritance, still in force, had often created multiple divisions of individual plots and fields. The great majority of the agricultural land was still unenclosed on The Blayes, and divided in the medieval manner into strips, cattle being turned loose communally after the harvest. The original strips had been about a *bouveé* in area, the amount a single furrow ox-plough could cover in a day, and at each end there was a *vaindif* or turning space, about 3 ft wide, and a 3 ft *vaindivage* which constituted a right of way for access to adjoining strips.

At the Court of Chief Pleas, any member of the electorate could address the court on any subject of interest or make complaint, either about matters of personal concern, or on behalf of a group. In those days requests and complaints made at this time were usually discussed by the court, and frequently acted upon. The origin of this Norman custom is thought to be with the Court of Pleas to which the people came to render homage to the seigneur and pay their rents, tithes and other dues, at which time grievances were probably aired to the fee-farmer or his agent. All the ordinances made since the last session also had to be confirmed at these courts, which were also responsible for setting the value of the wheat rent for the year, the *Besoin Publique*, (a property tax) which was the only tax raised on the island for normal administrative needs, and the Poor Law tax, administered by the Poor Law board. Both the taxes were set at a few pence tax for each 'quarter of wheat' rental value of the property. A small road tax was levied on those whose property fronted a public road, yielding a total of about £38 a year. The *Impôt* or 'duty' on alcohol, tobacco, and tea, was the island's principal source of revenue. This was supplemented by the *congé* or tax on property transactions, part of the 'seigneur's' revenues until 1825 when it devolved to the Crown, on the hereditary governor, John Le Mesurier, surrendering his patent.

After each session of Chief Pleas, the entire administrative body was entertained by the Judge to a dinner at public expense, which the Procureur, Greffier, Sheriff, Sergeant, and Constables were also entitled to attend. For the unpaid elected members these two dinners a year represented their entire reward for their services.

Under the Judge, the day-to-day running of the island was carried out by a number of crown appointees. In 1939 the details of those appointees were as follows.

The Greffier (or Clerk of the Court): Charles Batiste, an untrained but competent lawyer, was paid the princely salary of £25 per year, and given a small six-roomed States' house attached to the Courthouse. He was responsible for recording all of the court transactions, and also all property transactions, and was required to furnish free of charge to all who requested them copies of relevant documents. He also received fees for acting as registrar, and a 5 per cent commission on the stamp duty on documents.

The court had unrestricted powers in dealing with civil matters, but was limited in criminal cases to dealing with those matters which did not carry a sentence of more than one month's imprisonment, or a fine of £10, or both. Beyond this, cases had to be dealt with by the Royal Court in Guernsey, and persons convicted in Alderney also had a right of appeal to the Royal Court.

Procureur du Roi, that is the Crown Prosecutor: R.L. Duplain.

The Sheriff or Prévôt: J.T. Pezet's duties included holding both realty or personalty as stakeholder, pending the settlement of property disputes, especially in disputes over inheritance. He was also responsible for conveying prisoners to and from the court and the safe custody of the island's standard weights and measures.

The States' Treasurer: A.C. Tourgis.

The Sergeant: J.J. Renier lived in a house attached to the Courthouse with the gaol at the rear.

The Jailer (HM Turnkey): J.J. Herivel.

The Constable: R. Allen's role was distinct from that of the policeman. His duties included an annual inspection on New Year's Day of the weights and measures used in all retail premises and public houses. The constable was elected annually in rotation, and replaced by one of his deputies the following year. In 1939, the deputies were J. McCarthy and E. Angell.

The police sergeant: Police Sgt. Pike was the paid representative of law and order.

Procureur des Pauvres: B.H. Osborne, the chairman of the Poor Law board, was responsible for the control and distribution of funds for the needy.

Jurats: D.S. Le Cocq, W.P. Duplain, A.C. Tourgis, C.G. Kay-Mouat, Capt. C.H. Richards and E. Parry.

Douzainiers: J.B. Simon (Dean), J.W. Parmentier, F.C. Odoire, T. Burland, H.R. Slade, H.N. Herivel, T. Herivel, C. Jennings, R. Cleal, Lt.-Col. F.W. Marriette, J.P.W. Sebire and J.D. Duplain.

The Crown Receiver: Lt.-Col. L.J.A. Langlois. He lived in St Anne's House, now the States' Offices, but at this time this was his family's private residence.

The other public officials were: Receiver of the *Impôt*, or duty, on spirits etc., P.D. Sumner (also proprietor of the Belle Vue Hotel); Harbour-Master and Customs Officer, F. Baron; Inspector of Explosives, B.H. Osborne.

Such was the state of things in 1940. After the war a new, written constitution of Alderney was prepared. Known as 'The Government of Alderney Law, 1948', it came into force on 1 January 1949. The Clerk of the Court was to take over the functions of Procureur du Roi, Greffier, Sheriff, and Sergeant, but the Court could appoint special constables to assist the members of the Guernsey Police on duty in Alderney. The Douzaine and the Poor Law board were disbanded. The Court and States were separated, each with their own 'clerk'. The office of Judge disappeared, the head of Alderney's civil administration becoming an elected President with a States of nine elected members, later increased to twelve. The Chief Pleas continued to be held twice a year before a States' meeting, and law was to be administered by a bench of six unpaid, appointed Jurats, with the senior Jurat acting as Chairman of the Bench.

Since the construction of the breakwater and forts in 1847–55, a garrison of regular troops had been maintained continuously in Alderney. The British Government had withdrawn the garrison in 1929–30, and this had much reduced the island revenues. Following this, several of the chain of Victorian forts ringing Alderney had been bought privately at an auction held in 1930, mostly for ridiculously small sums of £30 or less, and were occupied as private dwellings or flats. Forts Tourgis and Albert had been retained by the War Office and had resident caretakers. They were still in occasional use for scout and guide camps, and by visiting army units from England. Fort Grosnez was retained by the War Department, Ministry of Works for breakwater maintenance, and the States had leased Fort Corblets to Francis Impey. The Nunnery also still belonged to the States.

In 1939, although the largest number of actual workers were engaged in 'trade', the principal industry of the island was still granite quarrying, both for export of crushed roadstone and cut blocks, and for the maintenance of the breakwater, which was still owned and maintained by the Crown. The Channel Island Granite Company employed nearly one sixth of the island's adult population, amounting to almost one third of the island's actual work-force. The 'crusher' at Braye harbour was consequently kept fully occupied with a continuous stream of boats arriving to collect the roadstone. Among these were the motor vessels *Ngaroma* and *Ngatera* plying out of Littlehampton.

At this time, too, there was little waste land in Alderney, about half the total area of the island being under cultivation, and a thriving trade existed in new potatoes for export in May and June, with other root and vegetable crops contributing during the year. Bulbs were grown for the cut-flower trade. Most of the hay and cereals needed in the island for cattle feed were home produced, and there was a steady export trade of Alderney cattle, which fetched good prices in both England and America. The Royal Alderney Agricultural Society held a regular cattle show and fair on the second Thursday in July which attracted many visitors, especially from Guernsey.

Much of the cultivation was done by smallholders, many of whom worked in the quarries during the day. Some of the family lands had been acquired in the general distribution of Common Lands in 1830, although by this time they, too, were much subdivided by inheritance.

The remaining employment in the island was divided between a variety of occupations. Fishing and work at the small-scale gravel works at Platte Saline accounted for some. A small building trade also existed and there were various craftsmen. There were twenty-seven 'professional' people – doctors, teachers, nurses, and so on –, thirty-one States' employees, and, increasingly, since the opening of the airport in 1935, a number working in tourism, including the hotels. A tourist office was maintained in the States' building, and a guide book to Alderney had been printed, and was being revised regularly.

Access to Alderney was provided both by the regular air flights of Jersey Airways, using de Havilland Rapide biplanes, and by sea. There were three boats

Airport manager Wilma le Cocq, September 1939

a week from Guernsey (or more depending on the season), the run usually being performed in about two hours by the SS *Courier*, the island's regular supply boat, which also brought the mail and the Guernsey and English papers. Other vessels regularly involved were *Joybell*, *New Fawn*, *The Guernseyman*, and *Glen Tilt*. Quite frequent excursions to Cherbourg were available, the ships of the St Malo and Binic Steamship Company calling in *en route* between Guernsey and Cherbourg. The *Courier* also advertised occasional trips to Cherbourg. In 1939 passenger boats from Weymouth and Southampton were also running regularly to Guernsey and Jersey.

Kelly's Directory for 1939 notes that The Guernsey and Alderney Trading Co. Ltd ran vessels to Guernsey and Portsmouth on Tuesday and Friday, returning on Wednesday and Saturday, and that Sark Motor Ships Ltd vessels made the journey to Guernsey daily in the summer and thrice weekly in the winter.

The principal hotels at that time were the Grand (built in 1936 as the Blue Horizon) with twenty-nine bedrooms, Riou's (now the Georgian), the Belle Vue, the Marais Hall, and the Victoria. There were also a number of private guest houses.

Visitors and islanders alike could enjoy the peace and charm of Alderney, and at the same time their recreational needs were met by various facilities. Swimming was available at several excellent beaches and at the Grand Hotel pool. A nine-hole golf course, originally set out by the army, existed along the slopes of Fort Albert towards Saye Farm, and visitors could use the club pavilion for 1s. 6d. a day (7½p). Visitors were also welcome at the cricket club. There were hard tennis courts for hire behind the Duplain's Riduna House in Victoria Street and at Val des Portes, then in three flats, but now the president's private house, with grass courts available at Sauchez House and in The Trigale. The peace of the public gardens in The Terrace, given to the island by Judge Barbenson, could be enjoyed. There was a regular, hourly bus service round the island from The Butes, and buses and the two taxis met all incoming steamers.

Entertainment was provided by several public houses and The Rink cinema at the junction of La Grande Rue and Le Val. The cinema was also used for dances and concerts by the Alderney Orchestra and visiting concert parties, and belonged to a company with the grand title of The Alderney Picture Palace Company. The old disused militia arsenal in Ollivier Street was also used for dances. The recently erected Grand Hotel provided entertainment during the season with a resident pianist, visiting artistes, and regular dances. Whist drives were held every fortnight at the Marais Hall Hotel. The Salvation Army provided a regular Sunday morning attraction on The Butes with its brass band.

The superb scenery and a wealth of wild flowers, birds, insects, and marine life, some few of them unique to Alderney and several others extremely rare in

England, attracted many naturalists and walkers. In contrast, the 'olde worlde' charm of St Anne, with its cobbled streets and fairly primitive (at that time) facilities, held considerable appeal over its visitors.

Lighting in the majority of the streets and many homes was by gas, with an efficient coal-operated gas works at the bottom of the Water Lanes. The bar of the Harbour Lights Hotel with its curved walls now occupies the site of the gas-holder. The small direct current electricity plant, erected on The Blayes by The Alderney Light and Power Company, was run by Alec Avis and had a fair distribution in town, which included electric lights in Longis Road installed in 1937. The other station at the back of the stone crusher installed by the granite company, primarily for their own use, also supplied alternating current to a limited area around Crabby Village and Braye. A few of the larger establishments, like Forts Corblets and Clonque, and the Drewitt's (Seymour House) in Connaught Square (later to become the Royal Connaught Hotel), had their own generators.

There was no proper piped water supply, and most homes had either their own wells or rain-water collecting tanks, the remainder relying on the public pumps from which they carried their water, a function usually allocated to the children of the family on their return from school each day. These pumps were located at Marais Square, Sauchet Lane, Les Rocquettes, in Le Vallée by the entrance to The Terrace, at the junction of Braye Street and Lower Road, at Simon's Place, at Sharp's Farm, and at Coastguards where there were two. There were also a number of places where small streams ran into troughs and a spigot was provided at which buckets could be filled. These were found at Judge Barbenson's fountain, Pont Martin, Crabby, Platte Saline, and in Valongis. Scattered round the island, including several along the south coast road, were a number of spring or stream-fed drinking troughs for cattle, *abreuvoirs publiques* (public drinking troughs), and three public wash places or *lavoirets* by the streams at Valongis, in Bonne Terre, and at Ladysmith. The latter, which is still in existence, was probably so named to commemorate the relief of its namesake in the Boer War, although the name may possibly be a corruption of the old words *les douits*, used in Alderney to describe such places but which in the other islands simply meant a small stream or running ditch, usually man-made. Cattle, which had by law to be tethered, were brought daily to drink at one of the dozen or so cattle troughs around the island, installed in Victorian times. Most are still in existence, the largest of which may be seen in Marais Square.

The sewers had been installed in Victorian times and most town houses were connected to them. Outside the town area, however, most homes still used earth closets, while a small number had cesspits.

Communications were limited. The island was connected to the mainland by a radio telegraph in the post office. This was a recent replacement for the undersea cable, sometimes out of action for weeks when it was damaged by friction over underwater rocks, by trawls, or by anchor cables. The post office was in the building which is now Riduna Stores (Le Riches). Captain Marriette was the regular postmaster and the telegrams were delivered by a boy on a bicycle. There was a very limited telephone service within the island. Some homes had a battery radio set and a very few had mains-operated sets, but news was still regularly disseminated by the town crier.

In addition to the Alderney news carried in the Guernsey papers and delivered regularly by SS *Courier*, there were two 'roneoed' publications in Alderney. Ian Glasgow published the weekly *Alderney Times* whose title and price varied from time to time. It comprised news, adverts, drawings and cartoons, tide times, shipping news, and satirical comment which on occasion landed him in court for contempt. Sometimes typed, sometimes handwritten, but produced entirely by himself on a duplicator, Glasgow's paper was published in Victoria Street on Saturdays, and usually priced 2d. It consisted of eight single-sided pages in a foolscap size. Glasgow lived and had his 'printing press' in the house on the site of the old Scott's Hotel, which had been burnt down in about 1924.

G.C. Price's journal, again produced on a duplicator, this time at Coastguards, was published on Fridays, in quarto format, and was also sold for 2d. *The Alderney Weekly News*, a typed paper with handwritten headlines and adverts, consisted of eight quarto pages, printed on both sides. The centre pages were devoted to 'Visitor's News', details of some of the personalities currently in the island, and contributions from visitors.

The summer season of 1939 was drawing to a close with the news getting gloomier day by day. For a time a detachment of the 1st Battalion, the Irish Fusiliers had been in residence at Fort Tourgis, but had left Alderney in June. When war was declared on 3 September, the island was once again defenceless.

CHAPTER ONE

War Begins

Hitler attacked Poland on 1 September 1939. War was declared on 3 September, a Sunday morning. Most of the remaining visitors in Alderney left soon after the announcement and a number of the young men of the island left to join the British Forces. By ancient custom the men of the Channel Islands are only required to give military service if led by the sovereign personally in any campaign carried on for the recovery of territory of the Crown, or for the rescue of the person of the sovereign if captured by an enemy. Nevertheless, in the 1914–18 war most of the men of military service age in the islands had joined up, and from Alderney forty-seven men lost their lives in the conflict.

On the day that Hitler moved into Poland an Air Raid Precaution (ARP) Committee was set up in Alderney, with Jurat C.H. Richards as its president, and Jurats D.S. Le Cocq, E. Parry, C.G. Kay-Mouat and W.P. Duplain as members. The secretary was W.J. Horton, and the vicar, the Revd H. Cooper Anderson, was appointed as chief warden. Meetings were held daily at the vicarage for the first sixteen days, while decisions were made about the provision of gas masks, since such attacks were feared. A decontamination unit in case of mustard gas was to be set up at the Mignot Memorial Hospital under the three doctors, A.S. Fletcher-Jones, H.R. Ramsbotham, and I.P. Moore, fire-fighting equipment and other supplies purchased, and seven posts were to be established around the island. The installation of an electric air-raid siren was much under discussion, meantime the old church bell would be used, as it already was in cases of fire.

Black-out regulations were brought into force on the second day. There was already a new, motorized, fire-fighting pump apparatus held in charge at Fort Albert, and arrangements were made for a Mr Giles to come from Guernsey to demonstrate it, and the other equipment. By 6 September 400 large, 850 medium, and 100 small gas masks, and 40 respirators suitable for babies, had been ordered, and stretchers, fire-fighting stirrup pumps and axes had arrived. There was considerable discussion as to who should pay for the gas masks, which arrived a couple of days later at a total cost of £279 9s. 1d., and most were distributed within a few days. On 20 January 1940 the States passed an ordinance decreeing a fine for anyone who lost or damaged their civilian respirators, or who lost fire-fighting equipment. The final decision as to the individual's purchase or contribution has not been recorded in the committee's minutes.

On the fifteenth day Capt. Rapson of the small garrison reported that the first-aid post established at the militia arsenal in Ollivier Street was now fully equipped. The next day Capt. McMullen of the Royal Engineers (the REs) was asked to allow the RE Office at Braye to be used as another first-aid post, and the quotation for supplying the siren was accepted. Meetings of the committee were then reduced to about one every two weeks, or as required.

On 12 October a message came to say that the siren was on its way, and it was delivered two months later on 14 December. A decision was made to try it out on top of the Belle Vue Hotel and on the old church tower, to see which was most suitable, but a dispute then arose as to whether this was the siren actually ordered or a smaller, cheaper one. It was not until 25 May 1940 that the States' Treasurer, Peirson Sumner, was asked to investigate the correspondence to confirm the arrangements, and meantime the invoice for £17 was not to be paid. That date is the last meeting of the committee recorded in their minute book, and it seems likely that the siren had not been erected or paid for by the time the island was evacuated a month later.

The Royal Alderney Militia had been disbanded in 1929 when the garrisons started to leave the islands and so none of the young men in Alderney had any military experience. Several volunteered shortly after war was declared, before compulsory military service could be introduced. More joined the services after the evacuation and during the 1939–45 conflict twenty-five lost their lives.

The withdrawal of the garrisons in 1929–30 inevitably meant a large drop in the revenues of the island, and of the people, for the next ten years. The Sherwood Foresters spent a short time here in 1935, and the 1st Battalion, the Irish Fusiliers, had come to Alderney on an extended training exercise late in 1938, departing in June 1939. Shortly after the war began, towards the end of September 1939, the military returned to the island when a training unit of the Machine-Gun Battalion was sent to Alderney as a garrison. Forts Albert and Tourgis were opened up again, repairs carried out and a mass of stores and equipment moved in.

The Machine-Gun Training Centre consisted of 100 Territorial officers and Royal Army Reserve members from several different machine-gun regiments. They came to Alderney in the SS *Courier* after spending a few days in Guernsey. Maj. J. Harley (Captain at the time) recalls that the officers were taken to the Grand Hotel which became their mess, and the troops also put Château à L'Etoc in order for their own use. They had only one old staff car, brought from Jersey for the Commanding Officer, Col. P.R. Worrell CBE, DSO, MC, of the Devon Regiment.

Over the next month a further 100 experienced officers and men, plus an assortment of vehicles, arrived and a month later the first intake of 200 recruits arrived in two batches of 100 men, the maximum *Courier* could carry at one time. These monthly intakes continued to a total of 800 recruits, by which time they occupied Fort Albert, The Arsenal, Fort Essex, and lastly Fort Tourgis. The old married quarters at Simon's Place, Whitegates and Coastguards were taken over again, and the extra 1,000 men placed a considerable strain on the island's resources to repair buildings and roads, find accommodation for the islanders displaced from the married quarters, and provide food. At the same time, of course, the two units had brought a degree of prosperity back to the island, and the shops were once again well stocked.

Capt. Harley was sent over to Fort George in Guernsey in February 1940 to establish a depot company for the training centre, to prepare the trained recruits for active service in a unit.

Over the next few months people, mainly the immigrants with families in the United Kingdom, left the island in small numbers. The 'phoney war' period which followed Hitler's forces sweeping across Poland, had hardly seemed to touch the islands. The air attack on Britain, expected hourly, did not materialize, German forces stopped at the Maginot Line and did not cross into France, and Russia occupied Eastern Poland. After some consolidation, and while the British were still debating whether to seek an alliance with Russia to prevent German expansion eastward, Russia annexed Latvia, Estonia and Lithuania. Finland would not accept Soviet control and was invaded on 30 November 1939, an action which caused the League of Nations, which had ignored Hitler's invasion of Poland, to expel Russia from membership. The Finns resisted and temporarily defeated the Soviet forces.

The French and British debated whether to assist Finland by taking an expeditionary force across Norway and Sweden to reach Finland, but when this plan was put to those governments, and they were invited to take part, in January 1940, they refused. The Allies decided to go ahead and do it anyway, but while preparations were still being made the Finns agreed to the Soviet demands on 12 March 1940. As had been the case with Poland, although war had been declared by Britain and France as a result of that invasion, no actual help in the form of men or munitions had been given to Finland. Furthermore, on 8 April, while the Allies were still debating a project to mine the Baltic and deny it to both Russian and German shipping, Hitler invaded Denmark and Norway, the German forces were unopposed, and occupied every important

Norwegian port from Oslo to Narvik and most of the Norwegian airfields, in the matter of a few days.

This time the British Government did respond to Norway's appeal for help. The result was a fiasco, but eventually Narvik was captured on 28 May (and evacuated again on 8 June). During this operation a British aircraft carrier and two destroyers were lost, but the greatest part of the German Navy was also put out of action, at least temporarily. The principal result of the failure of the Norwegian campaign was that Winston Churchill had replaced Neville Chamberlain as Prime Minister on 9 May. The next day Hitler invaded Holland and Belgium without any warning. The Allies sent troops into Belgium and Holland (by this time there were ten British divisions in France on the Western Front), but to little effect, and Holland capitulated on 15 May. The French 'impregnable' Maginot Line did not reach the sea and the German armies simply swept round the end of it and cut off the British army in Belgium, which country capitulated on 28 May. The evacuation of the British troops from Dunkirk had begun the previous day and was completed by 3 June with nearly 350,000 men being brought off, but not without the loss of 68,000 British soldiers, 474 planes, 6 destroyers and virtually all the troops' arms and equipment.

A few Alderney stalwarts had wanted to take Judge French's fast motor yacht to Dunkirk to help in the evacuation, but this was not permitted them. *Sea Salter*, however, a boat bought after the war by local diver Ron Smart, which then spent many years in Alderney as a salvage vessel, did take part in this operation and had a plaque recording the rescue of 450 men affixed to it.

There was now nothing to prevent Hitler's forces sweeping across France, and on 18 June Churchill warned the British people that an attack was imminent, in his famous speech containing the sentence, '. . . if the British Empire and its Commonwealth last 1,000 years, men will still say, "This was their finest hour". . .'.

CHAPTER TWO

The Evacuation

By mid-June 1940 when Hitler's invasion of Europe was sweeping across France, there seemed little hope that Alderney, third largest and most northerly of the Channel Islands, would be able to defend itself against the victorious German Armies. Situated as it was only about 9 miles off the coast of France, it had just the small garrison of the Machine-Gun Training Centre, mostly raw recruits, and a population of about 1,400 civilians to see off any attack.

The island, so strongly fortified against possible invasion by the French at various times since Elizabeth I and again during the Napoleonic Wars, could not hope to withstand the weapons of modern warfare, and the vast numbers of troops available to the enemy. The island lay within such close proximity to France and the long-range guns, and German air power was so superior at the time, that even the mighty Victorian forts ringing the island, and its huge Harbour of Refuge, could not guarantee its safety. Neither could the island have been kept supplied with food and ammunition had it resisted.

By now the Germans had reached Paris, declared an open city, and were advancing on Cherbourg and on down the coast to St Malo. On 15 June it had been decided to withdraw the Machine-Gun Training Centre from Alderney and divide it to defend the airports in Jersey and Guernsey. Capt. J. Harley was over in Guernsey supervising the battle training of the recruits sent over from Alderney after their arms instruction.

Another young officer here at that time, John Everett, who kept a diary of daily events, noted that on Saturday 15 June 1940 he was orderly officer and spent the morning supervising the laying of another telephone line from Fort Albert to The Arsenal. He:

> visited Château à L'Etoc to inspect lunch and tea meals, and during the evening paid two visits to the airport at 9 p.m. and midnight to check that all was quiet, despite the depressing news of the French collapse.

The following morning, Sunday 16 June, at 6 a.m., he met the RAF high-speed launch at the harbour, which brought news that the troops in Alderney were to be evacuated immediately. Capt. Harley confirms that orders were received in Guernsey late on Saturday evening, to move the machine-gun centre from Alderney, and to use these troops to defend Jersey and Guernsey airfields. Some troops were taken off on *New Fawn* within a few hours of the order arriving, and Everett noted in his diary:

> . . . The MG companies went today, one to Jersey and one to Guernsey, and at L'Etoc we got all packed up and ready to leave tomorrow. We saw the *New Fawn* leave, weighed down to the Plimsoll, maybe they'll get there by 1 a.m.

This departure removed any hope which the people may have held of Alderney being defended, and deep depression followed. One islander wrote in England, a couple of weeks later:

> . . . troops, our troops! Running away! Boats of every description appeared almost from out of the skies to take them . . . , did we panic? NO! The church services were held as usual and the people remained calm . . . Later we sat on the cliffs and waited for a boat – for help – for news.

Everett's diary continues:

The main body of troops left around midday on 17th, sailing along the side of Sark to Jersey on SS *Joy Bell*, a further party left on the morning of the 18th June . . .

John Everett saw *New Fawn* arriving with this party, at St Helier at about 11 a.m. He went to the harbour to help unload, and to recover his bicycle. He spent the day helping the unloading, and guiding officers and men to their billets. On the same day, *Courier* took the families of the soldiers to Guernsey. Churchill made his stirring speech to the British people the following day, but by then the decision had already been made to demilitarize the Channel Islands. Everett recorded in his diary:

> On the morning of 19th, the Jersey party received orders to reload all the stores and depart for England. In an atmosphere of chaos SS *Malines* left with part of the unit and stores, she left only 3/4 loaded, the Jersey Militia evacuated on *Hodder*, and boatloads of civilian refugees were leaving. The ferry *Autocarrier* came in, stayed an hour, and went with only about 40 passengers and none of the transport. The train ferry arrived at 10 a.m. and loading of stores and trucks continued until after midnight.

They finally left Jersey at 8 a.m. on Friday 20 June 1940, the last military to leave, and with scores of refugees on board, arriving at Southampton about 8.30 p.m.

Meanwhile, in Alderney, the last party had left in SS *Courier* on Wednesday 19 June, leaving large quantities of stores, vehicles, fuel, food, and the equipment for a complete military hospital on the quay; all the movable barrack equipment was locked up in Fort Tourgis. By the time they reached Guernsey, the order to evacuate the Channel Islands on 20 June had arrived and they were transferred at 5.30 the next morning to SS *Biarritz* which left at 8 a.m. leaving most of the equipment behind.

In Alderney, following the arrival of several boatloads of French soldiers and sailors fleeing from Cherbourg, where the Germans were now in possession, Judge French ordered all of the equipment and stores abandoned on the quay by the departing troops, except the food, to be destroyed.

The Guernsey Attorney-General, Mr Ambrose Sherwill, sent SS *Sherringham* to Alderney on 19 June, to offer passage to Guernsey to the school children and their teachers, and the remaining men of military age. The sisters from the convent with a number of children from there and from the public school, and just a few islanders, took advantage of this and left Alderney. Another ship, *Glen Tilt*, took off the French troops.

On the same day the UK Government went ahead with the demilitarization of the Channel Islands. However, it was decided to keep this secret, to avoid spreading alarm in the UK, and not to inform the Germans in case they took it as an invitation to take over. As a result, on 28 June, the German Air Force bombed St Helier and St Peter Port, which by then were empty of troops, causing quite unnecessary civilian casualties – forty-four were killed, including four of the party who were disembarking at White Rock after rescuing the animals from evacuated Alderney. There was also some damage to property. Because of this raid, SS *Courier*, under Capt. James Ingrouille and with thirty passengers and a cargo of pigs from Alderney aboard, was beached at St Sampsons, and went on to England next day without being unloaded in Guernsey.

By this time communications with Guernsey were erratic, Alderney had had no mail for nearly a week, and the Lt. Governor, Maj.-Gen. A.P.D. Telfer-Smollett, CB, DSO, MC, a serving officer, was recalled to the colours. He was replaced by Maj.-Gen. J.R. Minshull Ford, CB, DSO, MC, who had left Guernsey on 21 June after only two weeks in office. The administration of the island remained in the hands of the bailiff, Mr Victor Carey, who was henceforth to act as the King's Representative.

Palls of black smoke could be seen over France, and fires at night, as oil stocks were burnt ahead of the advancing enemy. Gunfire could also be heard.

In Alderney, the terrible decision had to be made: either to stay and risk certain occupation and life under the Nazis, or to abandon home and possessions and seek refuge in England, whence the fight against Hitler could be carried on.

Judge French called a meeting of the States of Alderney at 9 a.m. on Saturday 22 June, and by 10 a.m. most of the island population had assembled on The Butes, where the judge addressed them from the back of a lorry:

> Men and Women of Alderney, I have called you all together to tell you that this island you love so well is in grave danger – How long it will be before the Germans land here, I do not know. . . . Men and Women of Alderney, as you value your lives, if the boat comes, you get on it, for it will be the last touch with the outside world you will get. It will be the last boat to reach this island. If help comes the church bells will ring, and every man, every woman must leave their homes and go. I shall go, but I shall be the last man to leave the island. Men and Women of Alderney, I shall remain with you until every man and woman is safely housed in England, and afterwards, some day, we shall return to our beloved island.

The decision was taken by a show of hands. It was decided to leave. They all sang 'God Save The King' and went home to pack their one suitcase.

The judge had sent a message by the Trinity House vessel *Vestal*, which had arrived on Friday 21 June to take off the keepers, their families, and pensioners from the Channel Island lighthouses, and had returned to Alderney early on Saturday to drop-off Nick Allen, the pilot. In his note, the judge asked the Admiralty to send ships to evacuate the inhabitants. The notice illustrated opposite was posted on the Courthouse door. The ships arrived the following day.

Unknown to the Judge, the British Government had already made arrangements to send ships, and the lookouts posted to watch for them, farmer Joe Burland and Norman Renier, found six small cargo ships already riding at anchor in the roadstead at dawn, around 4 a.m. the next morning. A message was sent to the bellringer, Charles Goodchild, and at about 6 a.m. the awful message rang out across the island.

Cattle, domestic animals and poultry were turned loose, some owners had the gruesome task of shooting their dogs and prize bulls, and the butcher and vet helped many of those who could not bring themselves to do it.

In a remarkably short space of time, valuables were collected or buried, Judge

French removed all the deposits from the banks, and the people made for the harbour. Only about twenty people, including some of the very old inhabitants, refused to leave their homes and stayed behind, and by tea-time, except for these, the island was abandoned.

The embarkation was supervised by Charles Richards and Fred Marriette, the first ship leaving by 10 a.m. on Sunday 23 June 1940, *en route* for Weymouth. All arrived without incident, the last docking before midnight. The first into port was the seemingly aptly-named mv *Stork*, carrying 400 people, including one of the three island doctors. Three babies were reputedly born during the crossing. This was actually just a good story prompted by the name of the ship, although two-week-old Francis Herivel and six-week-old Fleur Riou were on the ships, and three babies were born within two weeks of their mothers' arrival in England.

Thus began nearly six years of exile for most of the islanders, but that is another chapter in the story.

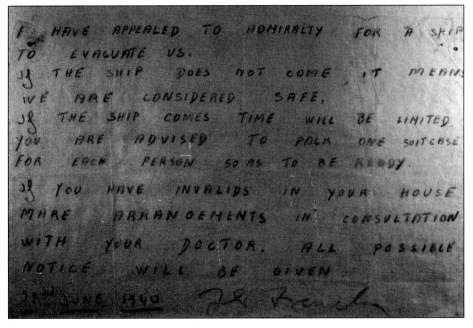

This handwritten notice was posted on the Courthouse door

CHAPTER THREE

Exile Begins

As the islanders sailed away to the north, to face they knew not what, so began a unique episode not only in the history of the Channel Island people, but also in the annals of all the British Isles. An entire population had voluntarily left their homeland. Alderney was deserted except for the animals and about a score of men and a few women who had refused to leave their homes, livestock, and possessions to the enemy, or who had been left with specific tasks to carry out.

Foremost among these was the Greffier, Charles Batiste, and his niece, who was married to Irishman Peter Doyle. James Alfred Rutter, a chiropodist, also

Peter Doyle dressed up in Hans Herzog's uniform at Lloyds Bank

stayed and was later imprisoned by the Germans for looting abandoned properties from which he had removed, among many other things, 20 pairs of ladies shoes and 200 sheets and other linen, probably from the shop premises of the Misses Martyn, on the corner of Victoria Street and New Street. The rest included Ernest Vincent Clarke, living in Val des Portes, farmer Frank Robert Oselton, Daphne Pope, her children, and her mother, Violet Gordon, 90-year-old Frank Le Cocq in Connaught Square, and brother and sister Clara and Jack Simon who were in their eighties. The old people were finally taken to Guernsey by a group sent over the following week to collect up the abandoned livestock and supplies. Several, including Frank, Clara and Jack, died in Guernsey during the occupation. Sidney Herbert Batchelor, who also lived in Val des Portes, happened to be in Guernsey at the time of the evacuation. Although his wife Julia had gone to England with the other islanders, he persuaded the Germans to bring him back to Alderney. George Pope and Peter Doyle were in Jersey, and were also brought back by the Germans. Many years later, London-born Elizabeth Jenkinson, who was working in Alderney at a hotel, claimed to have remained throughout the occupation. Her name does not appear in any of the recently released German records.

A few fishermen had remained to 'tidy up', including pilot John (Jack) Quinain and his two sons. Nick Allen went out to The Casquets lighthouse to destroy fuel stocks. He then left for England in his boat with his brothers Arthur ('Tim') and Richard. Arthur Jennings and his son, also Arthur, took official documents, the sub-postmaster R.P. Bury with his stamps and papers, and his assistant Mrs Honey, went to Guernsey. Capt. Marriette, the postmaster, had been recalled to the army on the outbreak of war. The Jennings then went on to England with F.L.J. Williamson and arrived at Teignmouth on 24 June. Pilot Daniel Ingrouille, 72 years of age, and 71-year-old Jack O'Connor also left in a small boat and arrived in Teignmouth on the same day. Some of the fishermen eventually went to England in their own boats. Ernest 'Bender' Audren left on 24 June and arrived at Dartmouth the next day, as did Benning Arnold. The Quinains went to Guernsey, where they spent the war.

In addition to the 1,432 Alderney folk, about one-half of the population of Guernsey and one-fifth of the Jersey inhabitants were evacuated in the second week of June. They included a large number of children and most men of military age, a total of about 30,000 people. Few left Sark.

The six ships carrying the islanders from Alderney arrived at Weymouth after crossings varying between six and twelve hours, on a flat calm sea and free from any attack by the enemy. The islanders disembarked and were taken to a nearby cinema and a school. Some were found overnight accommodation in houses and hotels, but the others slept where they were.

Next day they were taken to the station in buses. Those who had relatives to go to went off on various normal, very slow, stopping trains, taking, for example, twelve hours to reach Birmingham. The remainder were all put into one train and taken to Glasgow.

Throughout the war Mr Francis Impey, who owned Fort Corblets, kept in touch with all of the evacuees from Alderney through the Alderney Relief Committee, which later was associated with the Channel Islands Refugee Committee. Forms were sent out requiring details and valuation of all property left in the island at the time of the evacuation. The completed forms and the card index compiled by Mr Impey, which records details of changes of address, marriages, births, deaths, etc., are now kept in the Alderney Society Museum.

These cards and forms constitute a unique record of the island society in 1940 and a careful examination of them is almost like a looking into a miniature of the Domesday Book of England, which was compiled nearly 900 years earlier in 1086, but in quite different circumstances and for a very different purpose.

Few of us can imagine the anguish the islanders must have suffered at the time. Uprooted from their homes in an island which many of them had never previously left, they had to abandon almost everything they owned or held dear. They were forced to face an unknown future in, to many of them, an unknown land, and for no-one knew how long. The possessions of families some of whom had occupied the land for centuries, were all left behind except for what could be carried in a suitcase, or sack, and it is certain that few of them would have expected to see their treasured things or beloved animals again. Some items had been buried or 'hidden' and did indeed survive the war but that must represent only a small part of what had been abandoned.

By the time Impey had completed his survey in July 1943, the displaced islanders had settled in many areas of their new, albeit temporary, homeland. By then there were about 100 families living in London, south-east and east England, with 160 families in the west of England, the west Midlands and Wales, the largest number of these in the Birmingham area. There were a further 180 families in the north Midlands and northern England, with a number of the quarry workers having found work in the Lake District. Many of the Guernsey evacuees were sent to the Stockport area of Lancashire and about 200 families were in Scotland, mostly still in the Glasgow area. A number of the men and a few women had joined the British Forces.

Within a short space of time the officials from each community felt the need to preserve the links between the people and their homelands. The refugees from all of the Channel Islands were well catered for in this respect by the *Monthly Review* of the Stockport and District Channel Islands Society, which started publication in May 1941 as an eight-page leaflet. By January 1942 it had changed its name to *The Channel Islands Monthly Review*. It cost 3d. until the summer of 1942 when it was increased to 4d. (about 1½p). It then contained twenty-four pages and maintained this price until the last issue in August 1945, when all the refugees except the Alderney folk were being repatriated. News from and of the islands, messages seeking friends and relatives, and articles about the islands' history, geology and animals made up the content of each issue, so reminding the evacuees of their heritage. When the islanders returned home this publication was succeeded, in some measure, by the quarterly *Review of the Guernsey Society*, which has been published for members since 1945 by the Guernsey Society, based at the Royal Overseas League in London. The society is still based in London, meeting at The Architectural Association in Bedford Square. It acts as an organ of communication for Guernseymen and women all over the world, promoting the common interests of the Channel Islands. The Jersey Society in London was founded long before, in 1896, and its *Bulletin* fulfils the same function for Jersey expatriates.

CHAPTER FOUR

The Alderney 'Domesday Book'

In his summary of the completed census, dated 26 July 1943, Francis Impey detailed the steps taken to ensure the greatest possible accuracy of the records. (Impey was then head of the Kalamazoo Company in Birmingham, manufacturers of office systems, and by this time was providing employment to a number of the Alderney exiles.)

His opening statement is almost Churchillian in its statesmanlike approach to the situation, and its careful choice of words:

In June 1940 the people of Alderney retreated en bloc to England, to avoid the occupying German forces, and the English Health Ministry immediately came forward and gave aid and advice in providing hospitality during the time that Alderney people found homes and occupations.

The Alderney Relief Committee started, immediately they arrived in England, to work in the interest of the Alderney Refugees. This committee was, in the first instance, appointed quite informally; a few officials of the State of Alderney, and other people, all living near London, offered their services, and this group became the first Alderney Relief Committee. In February 1941, in order to improve the status and authority of the committee, the Alderney people 20 years of age and over, residing in England, were invited to vote in favour or against the appointment of the Alderney Relief Committee, to act in their interest during the period of evacuation. The vote of more than 700 people was over 99% in favour of the Committee continuing to act for them. In March 1943 Douzenier Lt.-Col. F.W. Marriette the former Postmaster, and Jurat C.G. Kay-Mouat were added to the Committee, as a result of a similar vote (and W.J. Horton as Assistant Hon. Sec.).

There are eleven kinds of forms and over 1,000 have been completed.

The original committee consisted of: chairman, Sir Henry Gauvain (a prominent Alderney-born surgeon); hon. sec., Capt. Charles Richards (States' official); Col. F.G. (Judge) French (head of Alderney's pre-war administration); Nicholas Gaudion (States' official); Mrs. P.C. Forsyth; Ernest Groom; Francis Impey.

After summarizing the results of the monumental task he had set himself, Impey notes that the completed forms appeared to have registered 100 per cent of the house property and land acreages which had been recorded in the 1939 *Kelly's Directory*, and 94 per cent of the population were accounted for.

It is interesting to note that he also summarized the methods of land measurement in use in Alderney, which differ somewhat from the English system.

Alderney measurements:

49 sq.yd.	=	1 perch
40 perches	=	1 vergée
2½ vergées	=	1 acre
1 acre	=	4900 sq. yd.

English measurements:

30¼ sq. yd.	=	1 rod, pole or perch
40 perches	=	1 rood
4 roods	=	1 acre
1 acre	=	4840 sq. yd.

The committee designed the eleven different forms to produce the best possible record of property abandoned, including the ownership of goods, buildings and land, the value of each item, and details of any insurance cover. The first batch was sent out in March 1942. When about half had been returned, the next batch was despatched, and so on. With all the necessary correspondence arising, the task was finally completed in June 1943.

The categories of form used and the numbers returned, were as follows:

1. House	Owner-occupier	195
2.	Tenant	278
3.	Owner-landlord	178
4. Trade premises	Owner-occupier	75
5.	Tenant	59
6.	Owner-landlord	37
7. Farms	Owner-occupier	55
8.	Tenant	69
9.	Owner-landlord	67
10. Fishermen		33
11. State, Church, Public or Trustee property		50

The details on the 1,096 returned forms showed that there were 514 dwelling houses, 1,432 inhabitants had been evacuated from the island, and there were 1,962 acres of land. The dwelling houses had 65 acres of garden between them, and also owned 60 acres of fields and 35 acres of rough grazing. The forms relating to the farm land asked for, among many items, details of the field names and areas, although many of these were incomplete.

The objectives of the survey were twofold:

1. To establish what was where in the island in order to enable the preparation of a plan for restoring the island when the islanders returned.
2. To then be able to claim compensation for whatever the Germans might have destroyed or removed.

The breakdown of the various statistical information requested is enough to constitute an entire book on its own, aside from the books containing the various sorts of completed form. Some of the facts extracted by Impey, and others culled from the forms themselves, form a valuable record of the social structure of Alderney in 1939–40.

The evacuated population consisted of 502 men, 529 women and 401 children. The occupations of the adult population up to the time they left were as follows:

Occupation	Men	Women	Percentage of adult population
Professional	12	15	2.7
Farming	73	53	12.2
Traders	125	84	20.6
Hotel and public houses	14	18	3.2
Quarrymen and			
War Department	135	1	13.4
Domestic	0	22	2.2
States' workers	24	7	3.1
No occupation	73	359	42.6

These had owned and/or occupied the following premises: 81 houses with 4 rooms; 255 with 5–8 rooms; 122 with 9–12 rooms; and 25 with more than 13 rooms, including some of the hotels. (These figures include kitchens, washhouses etc.) There were also 23 War Department or Granite Company houses and Forts Albert and Tourgis. The Granite Company had another 6 houses used as stores, which were not included in the 'Tenants' list.

The average value of property abandoned inside the houses, per room, was: houses with 4 rooms, £30; 5–8 rooms, £35; 9–12 rooms, £45; 13 plus rooms, £65. The total value of this property came to £145,802, with a further £20,000 outside in sheds and garden stores.

The average value of the houses themselves was: houses with 4 rooms, £250; 5–8 rooms, £480; 9–12 rooms, £720; 13 plus rooms, £2,800. The total value of all of these came to £248,445.

Not all forms were completely filled in, but as far as they were, the information given about facilities such as lighting and water services revealed the following. (Note that no information was asked for concerning telephone installations.)

Lighting
186 houses had electric light, mostly in town, or at Crabby and Braye.
7 had their own generators.
152 houses had gas lighting, including some of the above.
257 houses used oil lamps, including many also included in the previous categories.

Water
116 houses had their own wells.
339 houses had rain-water cisterns, including many of the above.
The remainder relied on the public wells and fountains.

Sewerage
216 houses were connected to the main drains.
A small number had cesspits or septic tanks.

Toilets
285 houses had a WC, many of them outside.
108 houses had earth closets.

Baths
118 houses had a plumbed-in bathroom.

It will be noted that only about one-fifth of the houses had a bathroom at that time and about half had a flush toilet. The houses with these, in many cases, noted the installation of hand or, rarely, electric pumps to an overhead storage tank. Only four houses, the convent, and the larger hotels noted more than one WC on the premises.

Trade premises comprised 4 professional premises, 9 licensed hotels and pubs, 62 tradesmen's premises and 79 shops, plus 1 War Dept tradesman's premises. The value of these properties was £56,000, their contents and stock £71,000.

The 25 public buildings had 241 rooms between them and owned 9 acres of gardens and 9 acres of pasture and heath. Their value with contents was just on £100,000.

The total value of property, excluding land, left in the island was £715,874.

There were 200 'farmers'on the island, men and women, with 66 of them engaged full time in farming. The land used comprised:

Arable	777 vergées in	462 separate plots
Grass	1,627 vergées in	517 plots
Heath	334 vergées in	198 plots

There were also 49 lots of common land.

Livestock noted on the survey forms amounted to:

41 horses; 277 cows/bulls; 234 heifers; 233 pigs; 129 piglets; 75 sheep; 100 lambs; 7 goats; and 4,373 fowl.

There were only 2 farmers whose stock was valued at more than £2,000, and 8 with £1,000–£2,000 of stock. There were only 2 holdings farming more than 200 vergées, and 4 others with between 100–200 vergées.

Of the land used, the 66 full-time farmers used a total of 1,050 acres for farming or market gardening. The remaining 134 part-time farmers held only about 75 acres between them.

The size of many of the plots of ground cultivated was very small, again due to the break-up of ownership, and a single holding was often rented from a dozen or more people.

The overall land usage of the island, in acres, was:

Land Usage	Acres
Houses and their gardens and land	160.8
Trade premises	7.5
Farms	1,126.5
States' and public spaces	19.0
Common land, foreshore and islands	165.7
Roads (14½ miles)	47.5

Fields rented to Jersey Airways were noted on several forms, so it is presumed that the land then occupied by the airfield was included with the farm land.

Motor vehicles left behind by the civilian population consisted of 28 lorries, including 13 Chevrolet and 9 Ford, 4 buses, and 73 motor cars of various horsepower. This last category divided into 14 Morris (mostly 8hp), 6 Ford, 16 Austin (mostly 7hp), 5 Essex, 3 Lanchester, 7 Standard, 4 Hillman, 1 Daimler, and various other makes. There were also 3 tractors, a Fordson, an Allis-Chalmers and one other, and 29 motor cycles including 16 BSA, 2 Triumph and 1 JAP.

Although 6 fishing boats were taken to England, a further 37 were left behind along with 25 other boats, mostly dinghies and punts.

Of all the forms sent out, only twenty-eight were not returned, although attempts were made to secure the missing ones, and several reminders sent out. This in itself is a tribute to the persistence of Impey and the others involved. A few forms were returned incomplete or not filled in at all. Despite the fact that compulsory education had only been introduced in the island in 1924, the last place in the British Isles to do so, only one of the forms was signed with an 'X, ** his mark', and the vast majority of the forms had been completed in the owner or occupier's own handwriting. It should be noted that the property of the people who went to Guernsey, the very few who stayed in the island, and a few who went overseas was not included in the survey. Any houses and land which had been occupied by these people as tenants would, however, have been recorded by the owner.

Naturally the owned property of those few remaining in the island was also not included, although in a number of cases returns were made by wives or other members of the family who had gone to England.

With these probably minor exceptions, which may affect the numbers of dwellings slightly, and the total value of the property by a relatively small sum, the figures quoted represent the entire value of Alderney in June 1940, apart from the land itself.

Impey comments in his notes that there appeared to be only a few cases of exaggerated valuations being given, and a far greater number of properties, goods and chattels undervalued. It is interesting to note the fairly small proportion of personal property which was covered by insurance. The principal exception to this was in the owner-occupied properties, and all of the public buildings. Just over half of the privately-owned buildings, and all of the public ones, were covered by fire insurance.

From detailed examination of these records, it would appear that very little was forgotten by the organizers in the preparation of the forms, even the rents paid or received for rented premises and land were included. Addresses given by those who completed them were probably those they used for mail. As the postmen usually knew everyone in the island, street names were probably sufficient for this, and they rarely included any house number or name. Only a few of the houses in town were named on the forms, making it a difficult task to positively identify the property concerned today. There was very little detail about the addresses of rented-out properties in the owners' summaries, especially for commercial premises. In trying to establish what shops were where, the memories of some of the surviving pre-war adults were helpful.

A good number of the country properties, either destroyed by the Germans, or demolished or built over since the war, are also difficult to identify with certainty.

Although a few extra facts would have been interesting from the point of view of a sociological survey of island life half a century ago, much of the desirable additional information can be obtained from Impey's card index. This usually records relationships to other people, the maiden names of married women and widows, and the occupations of those who worked. The only things completely missing are the educational history and attainments of the individuals, and details of their recreational activities.

Persons completing the forms sometimes enclosed detailed lists of property left behind. In these, prominence was frequently given to pianos, sewing machines and especially wireless sets. A number of forms listed an Aga cooker, obviously a prized possession, three or four houses noted the number of electric points, and one house actually had an electric cooker, vacuum cleaner, food mixer, air-conditioner and washing machine, probably a rare occurrence considering the restricted electricity distribution of the time.

The electrical shops and several of the garages listed 'battery' or 'accumulator' charging plants, so it may be assumed that there was a fair demand for this service, almost certainly in connection with the LT side of the wireless sets of the period.

Significant, too, of the period was the small number of properties in Alderney with a bathroom. Several forms noted that a bath and the necessary fittings and pipes were at the premises, but had not yet been connected, perhaps indicating that the number of homes with this facility was beginning to increase.

Almost half (43 per cent) of the adult population consisted of retired people and married women who did not work, and children were almost one third of the total population.

The number of hotels and licensed public houses (nine), shows a very significant drop from the turn of the century when there were over thirty such premises. Today there are about fifteen.

For some reason which is not noted in the records anywhere, the premises and equipment of the Channel Island Granite Company, with probably the largest value of any firm in the island, were not included in the survey, although the personally-owned contents of those company houses which had been occupied were included by the tenants.

Of the bank premises, only those of the Westminster Bank are noted, and the Wolseley car belonging to this bank, used throughout the occupation by the German FK 515 commander, is not recorded anywhere.

Sgt.-Maj. Ertel and Cpl. Forst, 1941

CHAPTER FIVE

Commercial Alderney

From the information in the census forms, it would seem that there were many small businesses, some competing with each other in certain fields, especially food and domestic goods supplies.

The notes made on the various forms by both tenants and owners can be divided, as far as possible, into the following related groups.

Provisions

Bakeries	3
Butchers	2
Confectioners	4
Dairies	3
Fishmonger	1
Greengrocers	2
Grocery shops	16
Mineral water mfr.	1
Wines and spirits	2

Clothing

Boots and shoes	3
Boot repairers	3
Drapers	4
Ladies' gowns	1
Lingerie	1
General outfitters	3
Wool shop	1

Other commercial premises

Banks	3
Cafés	3
Chemist (pharmacy)	1
China, glass, etc.	3
Chiropodist	1

Coal merchants	2
Doctors	3
Electrical and radio	3
Fancy goods, perfume, etc.	1
Florist	1
Hairdressers (1 gents, 1 ladies)	2
Hardware and ironmongery	3
Musical instruments	2
Photography	2
Sports goods	1
Tobacconist	3
Toiletries	1
Toys, etc.	1
Watchmaker and jeweller	1

Craftsmen and services

Airways, Jersey (office)	1
Blacksmiths	3
Boat builder	1
Building and decorating	4
Cabinet-maker	1
Carpenters	3
Chandlery	1
Estate agent	1
Forage and corn mill	1
Garages and motor repairs	6
Haulage	4
Laundry	1
Lending library service	1
Mason	1
Newsagent	1
Printer	1
Stationery, books, etc.	2
Taxi	2
Undertaker	1
Upholsterer	1

Some few of these activities overlapped, and at least a couple of businesses had several adjoining premises, each selling a different range of goods.

CHAPTER SIX

Before the Enemy Comes

The enemy had not yet arrived in the Channel Islands, and on 25 June, the bailiff of Guernsey sent SS *New Fawn*, and SS *Courier*, the island's regular supply boat, over to Alderney. On board were a number of Guernsey farmers and members of the Royal Guernsey Agricultural and Horticultural Society, under the leadership of Mr Peter Mahy, who were to collect or destroy the livestock. They were accompanied by a St John Ambulance party, under Frederick Bush, whose mission was to remove medicines and appliances from the Mignot Memorial Hospital.

On arriving they apparently found evidence of looting in the shops, pubs and houses, and some animals still shut up in their stalls and half starved. The few remaining islanders did not appear to know what had happened. Animals were collected and dealt with, the badly suffering ones destroyed. Over the next three days 224 cows, 150 heifers, 5 bulls, 20 steers, 23 horses, 30 pigs and some carcases were taken to Guernsey. The cattle were originally taken to Guernsey Airport to graze, but when the Germans arrived in Guernsey a couple of days later, they ordered them removed, and they were distributed among the Guernsey farmers. A careful inventory was kept, and the value of the animals set aside, to be returned to the owners after the war. The sale of the animals realized £5,944 14s. 2d., after deducting 'expenses'.

The list of the other items officially removed from the island which were recorded and the value set aside in Guernsey makes interesting reading. The total value of the goods was £5,843 12s. 6½d., of which the principal items were, in round figures, £1,700 for coal, £1,000 for paint and ironmongery, £500 each for potatoes, groceries, agricultural implements, clothing, and engineers' stores and equipment. The remaining items included fuel oils, medical supplies, cereals and fodder, empty casks and barrels, other minor stores and 'Coffin sets, value £36 19s. 4d.'.

The accounts were finally made up by the Guernsey States Accountant and dated 16 February 1946. A charge of £1,722 0s. 10d. was made against the value of these items by the Guernsey Authorities for 'wages', £387 0s. 1d. for freight and cartage, £161 2s. 7d. for food, and sundry small items. Bearing in mind the average weekly wage in 1940 for manual workers, this charge seems vastly excessive for a few days work by about thirty men. The accounts do not show any interest on the balance of some £9,406 18s. 0½d. which had been held for 5½ years.

Guernsey agricultural workers *en route* to Alderney, 1941

The master of *Courier* had been given the keys of the church, to remove the plate and records. Time was also found to obstruct the airport runway with lorries and wire.

At the time of the final removal of livestock, all except seven of the remaining Aurignois were persuaded to leave and go to Guernsey, Charles Batiste and Frank Oselton being carried off at gun-point. (Oselton later persuaded the Germans to allow him to return to his farm and animals.)

A later result of the looting that had occurred was the trial of thirteen men accused of the crime of 'plundering'. The trial took place on 28 October 1941 in the Guernsey police court, under a military tribunal, the president of which was Dr Peyrer von Heimstaedt. The action was taken by the military authorities primarily to clear the name of the German troops, and because the Guernsey civil authorities, to whom the case had been handed in May, had done nothing in the meantime.

James Rutter, aged 67, of 37 Victoria Street, Alderney, a chiropodist, pleaded 'not guilty' and was sentenced to one year's imprisonment. Douglas Rihoy,

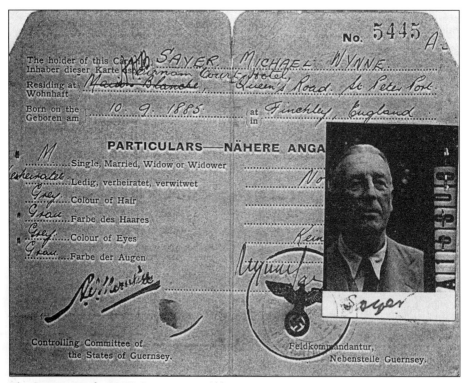

The German pass for M.W. Sayer to go to Alderney

Arthur Torode, Walter Guille, Clifford Bichard, William Oliver and Charles Hutchesson, all Guernsey residents, had indulged in somewhat more petty plundering during March and April 1941, and were sentenced to terms ranging from three weeks to two months. Six others were acquitted.

It was established that, later in the afternoon of the day the islanders left, a lifeboat with five or six French fishermen on their way to England, spent the night in Alderney and broke into 'Bucktrouts' for tobacco. Later, on 25 June, members of both the farming and Red Cross parties (a German description – they were actually St John Ambulance personnel) were seen to break into various clothing stores, jewellers and other premises in St Anne. On returning to Guernsey they took with them a great deal of baggage, probably containing the plunder. During the period these men were working on the island some of the crew of both *Courier* and *New Fawn* took part in this plundering and, it was said, both captains joined in and much more was removed.

In addition to the removal of goods and possessions, considerable damage was done to the houses and property – windows, doors and furniture were smashed, and things strewn everywhere.

J.A. Rutter's advertisement in the Alderney Weekly Times, August 1938

CHAPTER SEVEN

Swastika over Alderney

The abandoned island of Alderney was 'invaded' by the *Luftwaffe* which landed at the airport on 2 July 1940. Larger planes carrying troops, sent over from Guernsey, had to turn back, unable to land on the obstructed runway. Shortly after, two Fieseler Storch planes, which only require a short landing space, got in and their crews cleared the obstructions. The airport building at that time was a small wooden hut, until a couple of weeks previously the domain of Wilma Le Cocq (now Wilma Bragg), who had managed the airport single-handed except for the assistance of a groundsman, Sam Allen, who doubled as baggage handler. There had also been a tea-room managed by Mr and Mrs Toussaint.

The Germans found the island apparently deserted, the seven remaining inhabitants keeping out of the way. There was, of course, no resistance to their landing, nor to that of the sea-borne party from Cherbourg which arrived later in the day. The whole force of about eighty men was commanded by Sgt.-Maj. Schmidt, replaced a few weeks later by Sgt.-Maj. Koch.

The report of the occupation of the Channel Islands in the German newspaper *West-Front*, dated 29 July 1940, makes interesting reading:

. . . By the united strength of our Army, Navy and Air Force, the Islands of Jersey, Guernsey, Alderney and Sark have been taken. This is the first time in 1,000 years that the islands have been invaded.

The exaggeration of the force necessary to occupy four undefended islands, and the disregard for historical fact, is perhaps representative of the difficulty which was to occur over the next few years in obtaining reliable, accurate, and unbiased reports of events, especially from virtually abandoned Alderney. In this respect it seems reasonable to assume that the contemporary Guernsey newspaper reports of daily happenings are likely to be as accurate as can be found at this distance in time, and much use has been made of them.

The suggestion was made in Guernsey, and published in the papers, that many materials were likely to become short there, and that perishable goods, and particularly horse harness and equipment which had been left in Alderney, should be collected. The Guernsey Labour Department proposed an expedition,

WHO'S FOR ALDERNEY?

Some 20 to 30 Men Wanted for Salvage Expedition

It seems quite possible that, in a few days from now, an expedition of Guernseymen will sail from Guernsey for a few weeks' work there in the salving of island stores.

The proposition regarding this work is one that was made to Guernsey's Labour Department, directed by the Controlling Committee of the States of Guernsey, by the German Commandant here, and it was taken up at once by Deputy R. H. Johns, and by the Rev. P. Romeril, who is acting as Mr. Johns' personal sercretary, unpaid.

Interviewed this morning, Mr. Romeril said that he could not resist the thought that it had been a mistake to evacuate Alderney completely from the civic point of view. Rather, he thought, should a maintenance staff have remained there to keep things in an orderly way, and to generally watch over the interests of the evacuated Island.

With regard to the proposed expedition, some 30 men of a reliable type would be required, and it was hoped to have that number ready in two days from now. These should register with Mr. P. Honey at the Labour Bureau, States Office, North Esplanade, and the men forming the expedition would be selected from those registering for this.

The Rev. P. Romeril, who is the Methodist Minister at St. Sampson's, and is doing such valued work with Deputy Johns, was in France for five years in the last war, serving in the 55th Division, and was with the Army of Occupation in Belgium and district, and, in the course of his duties, had frequently to go in and out of Germany.

ALDERNEY MEN VOLUNTEERS?

Mr. Romeril observed that there were a number of Alderneymen in Guernsey, and the Authority would be glad to have their assistance in the work contemplated.

Such men could obtain an interview with Deputy R. H. Johns, at Elizabeth College, either to-day or to-morrow.

'Who's for Alderney?' – A cutting from the *Guernsey Evening Press*, 18 July 1940

published in the *Guernsey Evening Press* on the 18 July under the headline, 'Who's For Alderney?'. As a result, Alderney saw the arrival on 20 July, of a working party of about twenty men from Guernsey, travelling on the motor yacht *White Heather*, owned by Capt. T.A. Clarke, and accompanied by a small party of German officers and men.

Subsequent newspaper reports on this group of agricultural workers, originally sent merely to harvest the potato and other crops left by the departing islanders, and to salvage useful stores, vary a little on the names, especially the initials of those involved, but the first party was under the command of H. Perchard, with C.F.F.T.P. Le M. Hutchesson as second-in-command. The storekeeper was W.T. Oliver, and the cook T. Creron. The remaining workmen were J.W. Arkwright, C.J. Bichard, N. Breton, W. Brouard, W. Brown, G.W. Buckingham, D. Campbell, A. Dodd, W.D. Domaile, L.P. Green, W.R. Hamel, A.J. de Jersey, C. Madell, R.W. Miller, H.G. Le Noury and A. Torode.

A letter sent to Guernsey on 25 July by C.F. Hutchesson states,

. . . the German Commander is a very nice man, and has been exceptionally helpful and we are very happy.

By this time potatoes had been put in barrels for shipment and there were 20–30 tons of flour on the jetty waiting for a ship. On the same day (25 July) Alderney-born Sir Henry Gauvain, the eminent orthopaedic surgeon, spoke on the BBC feature programme *The World Goes By* to the exiled Aurignois. After describing the evacuation, for the benefit of all listeners, he finished his talk by saying in the Aurégny patois:

Alderney people, all goes well. Take courage. God is with us. We'll go back some day.

The speech was reported in the *Guernsey Evening Press* the next day. That day *Staffa* left for Alderney to retrieve the stores, taking mail, food and cigarettes for the men, a further ten workers, and a farrier, Mr Joseph Rowe, and his son, to shoe the horses.

A few days later, on 27 July, a letter appeared in the *Guernsey Evening Press* suggesting the setting up of a 'colony' on Alderney to look after the property, and preserve the abandoned houses. However, this appears never to have been taken up by the Controlling Committee, although over the next few months several groups from Guernsey went backwards and forwards to repair some of the damage to houses and collect useful materials and stores. There was a later report of 150 Jerseymen being sent over in mid-1941 to carry out further repairs

SS *Staffa* at Braye, 1940

to the houses. Recently released German records show that there were an average of about eighty men and a few women from Jersey and Guernsey continuously in Alderney until D-Day 1944.

On 29 July *White Heather* made a return trip to Alderney, and this was the start of regular sea connections with Guernsey, using *White Heather*, and the SS *Staffa*. The latter was sunk in Braye Bay on 13 March 1941, apparently being sabotaged by her own crew at the south-west corner of the stone jetty where she remained until about 1950.

At the beginning of August a small detachment of *Luftwaffe* signallers, comprising a corporal and twelve men, were sent from Guernsey to Alderney to act as plane spotters. They flew to Alderney via Dinard and Querqueville (a small airfield west of Cherbourg), arriving in a Junkers JU 52 on 2 or 3 August. The first troops on the island, they landed without difficulty at the airport, and were quartered at Fort Albert, although as yet there were no proper water supplies or food there. One of the party, Rudolf Hager, recalls that Sgt.-Maj. Schmidt was then Island Commandant, and they searched every house in St Anne for food, finding little. They hunted and 'killed a pig running wild, having been set free by the departing islanders', but 'emaciated, being unaccustomed to feeding itself'. They had at this time very little food and '. . . just had to smoke

THE FUTURE OF ALDERNEY

Sir,—It is heartening to read your accounts of the work of the men of the salvage expedition sent to Alderney. But why an expedition? Why not establish a society of colonists there, who would, in the spirit of good enterprise, settle down in the Island for the period of the evacuation, and, under the supervision of an appointed officer, labour there and so help to keep the Island going?

There is no such quick way to deterioration as letting an island go wild, and I am sure that a large number of Sarnians would be found willing to go there and work on the land if it were given them free for working. Quarters could be found for them, and even homes, with proper checks made by inventories of furniture and household utensils put into service. Few proprietors of abandoned houses would complain if their houses were occupied, for occupation would tend to keep them in habitable condition.

With a regular service maintained by the Staffa the scheme would be possible, and with Alderney put into food production, and cattle returned there, there is no reason why Alderney could not contribute splendidly to our much wanted supply of food.

I would suggest that the workers could well be maintained under the Labour Department of our Controlling Committee, and the community might become large enough to attract a doctor and a parson; in which case families might sojourn there.

I cannot resist the thought that the evacuation of Alderney was prompted under the shadow of the dark cloud of the unknown. But the occupation of these Islands has shown that there is a silver lining to the dark cloud. There is, in fact, such a silver lining that many of the Alderney evacuees in Scotland might well wish to be safe in Alderney, an open island, but now a "deserted village."

A LOVER OF ALDERNEY.

A newspaper cutting from the *Guernsey Evening Press*, 27 July 1940, suggesting that a 'colony' of workers be set up in the island

cigarettes as there was no meal for us'. There was a diesel generator left in Fort Albert which they used to power their radio transmitter and lights, and when it ran out of fuel, they dipped oil from the storage tanks at the Alderney lighthouse in buckets.

Hager continues:

. . . There was at least one old man left with white hair. He lived in the cellar of one of the houses in St Anne and came out of hiding with a pistol in his hand. [Could this have been Rutter?] When he saw we were friendly to him, he was to us.

I thought it a great misfortune at the time when we had to leave Alderney on 4 October 1940. But I now see how lucky I was, for I have been deeply shocked by the things which I now [1982] learn happened here later in the war. For myself, when I remember the seven years of war and captivity in the USA, I recall with happiness my two month stay on that beautiful island. I was 27 then and am now 69 and I thank God for health, strength and a little money now to have fulfilled my wish to see Alderney again.

Over the next few months frequent reports of the progress of the workers on Alderney appeared in the Guernsey papers. From these they appeared to be in good spirits, were well treated, and only short of cigarettes. As a result the press set up a cigarette fund for them, and was soon able to send sufficient on *Staffa's* weekly run to allow each man twenty a day.

A heavy crop of early potatoes had been lifted and sent to Guernsey, and a good yield of grain was to be threshed in Alderney to simplify transporting it. The Revd Philip Romeril, secretary to the Labour Department of the Controlling Committee in Guernsey, visited the island on 15 August. (The Controlling Committee had been set up at the beginning of the occupation in Guernsey to provide a quicker liaison between the civil administration and the occupying power than could have been provided by the States of Deliberation. With hindsight after the war, it might have been to the advantage of the island to have retained the somewhat cumbersome island administration, which could have effectively delayed the implementation of some of the German orders, as happened in Jersey.)

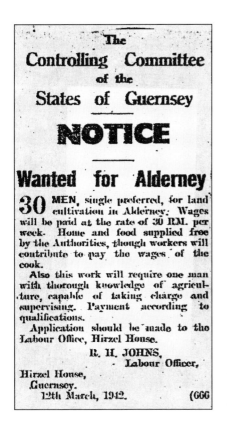

'Wanted for Alderney' – a cutting from the *Guernsey Evening Press*, 19 March 1942, requesting volunteers to work in Alderney

The Guernseymen were established in the Grand Hotel, where they remained until the entire party was withdrawn temporarily from the island in October 1942 after British commando raids on The Casquets and Burhou. During this time little restriction was placed on their movements, and they were well fed. A lively Christmas party was held in the hotel in 1940. At this time a 'newspaper', *The Alderney Times*, was started in December 1940. Produced on a typewriter by Neville Brouard as a single copy each weekend, it dealt purely with the activities of the Guernsey workers and included details of the work they were doing, personal comments about the members of the party, billiard and snooker scores, the results of competitions held between the groups, and a caricature.

Money was of no use in Alderney as there was nothing to buy, so the workers' pay was given, in part to their families in Guernsey, and the balance held for the men, against their return to Guernsey. Mail was regularly exchanged.

During 19 to 21 February 1941 a visit to the island was made by Councillor K.V.R. Pelz, the German agricultural officer in Jersey, and representatives from Guernsey, including *Sonderführer* (Special Officer) Hans Herzog, who was to play a significant role in the early years of the occupation. Following this visit a

Sonderführer Herzog out rabbit shooting, February 1941

decision was made to use 750 vergées (approximately 300 acres) of good agricultural land in Alderney to produce food, especially flour, for the German garrisons in both Alderney and Guernsey.

After the sinking of SS *Staffa* the service between the islands was carried on by the German motor vessel *Spinel* (a British vessel captured at Dunkirk, and finally scrapped in 1970), and a former Dutch vessel, *Elena*. There were also quite frequent visits from a larger ship, *Sperber*, with supplies from Cherbourg.

The Guernsey group was soon to be increased in May 1941, and later still, on 12 March 1942, an official notice in the Guernsey papers asked for a further thirty volunteers to work in Alderney at a rate of pay of 30 Reichmarks a week. (The 'official' rate of exchange at this time was about 7 Reichmarks to the pound, but the Germans worked on a basis nearer 4, when paying for items purchased from the local population in Guernsey.)

Also in May 1941 it was decided in Guernsey that the eggs from the gulls on Burhou would provide a valuable addition to the food stocks. An expedition was set up with Alderneymen Archie Sebire and Alfred Bideau, and Guernseyman D. Campbell. They left St Peter Port on 9 May, but owing to bad sea conditions were unable to land on Burhou, and returned the following day. The attempt was repeated on 31 May, reaching Burhou on *White Heather* and ferrying ashore in the motor boat *Ankiepilla*. This time they managed to land, but could only find two or three dozen eggs. The expedition was deemed a failure and the idea was not repeated.

The Germans turned the Convent into a soldiers' home in September 1941. The pictures of the exterior and interior, taken in 1942 for the small German guidebook to Alderney, *Die Inseln Alderney*, show that some considerable effort was taken to make this comfortable. The picture of Herzog's quarters in this building, taken earlier, forms a striking contrast. One member of the *Organisation Todt* (OT), *Hauptruppführer* Gustav Dahmer (q.v.), comments that, in April 1943:

> The Service library was excellent, not only did they have party literature, but good books which I frequently sent to the East front.

Also in September 1941 the trial, recorded in chapter six, took place of the men charged with plundering, the Guernsey authorities having failed to take any action against the persons concerned during the previous six months.

As far back as 9 December 1940, Capt. D. Bisset, who had accompanied the first working party under the charge of Mr P.A. Mahy sent over before the occupation, had written an account to the bailiff reporting the removal of over 300 head of cattle, and the humane destruction of many animals which had been

Der grosse Saal des Soldatenheims

The interior of the *Soldatenheim*, the pre-war convent which was turned into a social club and canteen for German soldiers

left shut up without food or water for six days. He notes that some shops were broken into by members of the party, but that he did not personally see any goods being removed. He also mentions that some Guernsey firms had sent representatives to remove stock from their Alderney branches, and that the St John Ambulance party was removing drugs etc. from the hospital as instructed. These obviously formed the basis of the items in the accounts noted in chapter six.

Capt. Bisset also states that Mrs Pope was still in the island, but returned to Guernsey with their party, and that the slaughtered animals were not buried because there was insufficient time.

In another report to the bailiff of Guernsey, from HQ Field Command 515 Jersey and dated 29 November 1940, Col. Schumacher, the commandant, records that most of the damage and looting had been done by the party sent over by the Guernsey administration, or by French fishermen. He cites Mrs Pope and Frank Oselton as witnesses to this, and goes on to say that much material had been removed by the 'English Working Party' prior to the arrival of the German forces. (His list also agrees closely with the items already noted.) Col. Schumacher also recorded that the *Inselkommandant* in Alderney had given

Col. Schumacher, FK 515, Jersey, in Alderney, May 1941

the agricultural working party permission, at their own request, to remove articles from their own and their relatives' houses, and to take them to Guernsey.

Several of those eventually charged with plundering were from the original party of volunteers, and others from the second batch, while Rutter had been an Alderney resident before the war. The newspaper reports of the proceedings with the names of witnesses called, create some confusion over the persons concerned. Presumably the second-in-command, C.F. Hutchesson (with six Christian names), who owned considerable landed property in Guernsey, and was sentenced to two months for 'persistent theft', was the same person as E. Hutchesson, described as 'The Civil Commandant'. If so, it was Hutchesson's own complaint of petty pilfering, made to the German authorities in April 1941, which led to the German field police searching the houses of remaining civilians. Plundered goods were found in the possession of several of the workmen, and both Hutchesson and several of his own men were consequently sentenced.

Rutter's house and shed at 37 Victoria Street was found to contain large quantities of foodstuffs, clothing, household articles, silver, cutlery, clocks,

Hans Herzog and German officials. C.F. Hutchesson is on the right

Customs Officer Rosemann, June 1941

carpets and furniture, tools, surgical instruments and medicines, agricultural implements etc. Further goods, including large quantities of household linens and twenty pairs of ladies shoes, were found at his other house, Capon Farm, Castel Hill, Guernsey, where he had taken them from Alderney. Despite the evidence, he pleaded 'not guilty' and tried unsuccessfully to explain his possession of the goods. His sentence of one year was reduced by three months for the time he had been in custody – in the circumstances a very light sentence.

After his first visit in February 1941, *Sonderführer* Hans Herzog, a civilian administrator and interpreter awarded this rank to give him authority, later commented:

> . . . the town of St Anne gave a completely neglected impression. The doors of the houses were open, all the windows were broken. The houses inside looked indescribable, furniture partly destroyed, drawers pulled out, the contents scattered about in the rooms etc. A picture of complete destruction. – Inhabitable were the houses of the Island Commando [the Guernsey Agricultural party], the house opposite 'House Keller' [the name of a German chief officer who lived there], 'Villa Brinke' and a few houses in Little Street, where the customs officer stayed . . .

The custom's officer was one Rosemann, about whom Herzog later comments 'he had nothing to do, but was always around'.

It was, of course, to counter suggestions that the German troops were responsible for this destruction and looting, that, on complaints of pilfering and desecration of the church being made by Hutchesson to Herzog, an investigation was made with the results already noted. It would appear, according to reports from George Pope, that up to this time the small party of Germans on the island had behaved correctly, although there were later reports of large quantities of furniture and household goods being shipped to Cherbourg, where they were possibly used to furnish the 709th Infantry Division HQ and the Naval HQ.

On 9 April Herzog, now the representative in Alderney of HQ 515 Civil Affairs Unit, at Grange Lodge in Guernsey, returned to Alderney in charge of the volunteers: farming, repair and working parties. Later, he visited the church with Hutchesson, found that it was being used as a wine store, and ordered the wine to be removed and stored in the gaol. He found himself a billet in a room in the convent, in considerable disarray when he arrived, and had his office in the military police HQ. at Lloyds Bank in Victoria Street. The bank soon became the *Austellen* (Out-station) HQ of FK 515, and the military police moved to The Jubilee Home in High Street.

Soldiers and their guests on the way to The Casquets for an outing, summer 1941

With his black dog, 'Lux', he spent much time walking round the island, taking photographs. During this period he kept a good but apparently fairly distant, relationship with the civilian workers until he was transferred to Jersey in May 1942.

In a report to his superiors, dated 10 February 1942, Herzog reviews the situation in Alderney since June 1940, made up from information he had collected since his arrival in the island a year previously. The first part of his report, based on evidence collected, confirms that dead animals were not buried by the Guernsey party, that French fishermen had earlier broken into the cigarette shop in Victoria Street, and that 'luggage' was taken to Guernsey. He goes on to say that the Pope family returned on 24 July 1940 with permission of the Island High Command, Guernsey, and found nearly all house doors and windows destroyed. At this time armed German patrols were in the streets to prevent looting, but soon had to be taken off in order to bury or burn the dead animals to prevent disease spreading. Herzog reports that Pope also told him that

Sonderführer Herzog, and his dog Lux, at the Old Harbour

the agricultural party (quote 'Working Commando') then living at the Grand Hotel, had done more looting and had taken or sent foodstuffs and furniture to Guernsey.

Herzog was supported by a police sergeant in charge of the police department, with three field-policemen, Sgt.-Maj. Oeser, Sgt. Ertel and Lisowsky. His report continues:

> . . . it was decided that an English working-party should be sent to Alderney to put the neglected houses in a decent state. As the work was urgent on account of the approaching summer, 50 workers from Guernsey were sent on 21 April and the work was started immediately.
>
> At the same time the work on the breakwater went on [as reported in the Guernsey papers, work had been started on maintaining the Breakwater by a 'British' working party, led by a harbour engineer on 9 April]. Stones had to be blasted, and this work in the quarry near the lighthouse had to be supervised. The work was finished on 8 September

German repair workers on the breakwater, 1942

1941 using about 7,800 tons of stone. The costs were taken care of by the States of Guernsey hoping to get these expenses back [presumably from the British Government] after the end of the war. The work of cleaning up the houses was accelerated and was finished after 30 days. The cleaning was not completely done as nobody knew then that it had been decided to increase the garrison of the island in a very short time. The electricity was looked after by the El-Dept of the island, run by soldiers. The El-Dept got the diesel oil from the infantry division, or from ships entering the harbour. But often one had to switch off the light as the stock got low.

The water supply was not much better. One cannot understand how the inhabitants in peacetime (about 1,500) could cope with this question . . . – In each household there is a pump, but only working when there had been rain . . . there is a very good fountain in a sidestreet off High Street (Sauchet Lane), and another one in Little Street giving good water during the whole year . . .

The pump in Sauchet Lane, from the 1942 Alderney guidebook

There was relatively heavy rain in 1941. The crops were partly flattened and could not be brought in quickly as the weather only improved in September. Nevertheless the English working-party succeeded in harvesting 180 ts. wheat. 65 ts. oats were given to the food office of the island for the horses of the soldiers and in addition also 40 ts. of hay and straw, the latter is carried away according to need. – The cattle consisting mainly of Guernsey cows which were brought here by order of the Island Command for the troops. The cattle belong to the States of Guernsey and are neither to be slaughtered nor brought to the mainland. There are 18 cows for this purpose. 1 cow belongs to the English working-party, the others are distributed to the units through the Island Command. Goats, pigs and chickens are also here, but except for the goats they belong to single units. The goats have remained from pre-war times. There are three horses belonging to the island. In addition to these the farmer Oselton of Mill Farm has got about 14 cows and 1 bull. There is also 1 horse. Farmer Oselton earns his living by selling the milk. His only help is Mr Clark.

Guernsey volunteers harvesting on La Petite Blaye, 1941

Nowadays we have a local farmer who has been appointed to look after the interest of the Air Command.[1] On the farm are 9 milch cows, 2 oxen and a few pigs. The soldiers' home has there installed its sheep and turkeys.

Long after the war, in January 1961, as a result of a picture of the Alderney locomotive *Molly* on the breakwater being reproduced in a German paper, Colin Benfield, the driver of the train, received a parcel containing 131 photographs taken by Herzog during his time in Alderney in 1941 and 1942. Some of his pictures are reproduced in this volume. After the war it was reported that Herr Herzog became a monk, overcome with remorse for the way in which his countrymen had behaved in Alderney. However, this was not mentioned in a letter written in English in May 1961 by Herr Herzog himself, and received in the island in October 1962, along with the copy (in German) of his original report of 1942.

The following extract is taken from Herzog's letter, reproduced exactly as it was written:

. . . when I entered the island on 19,2,1941, there were 80 soldiers of the army staying there, inclusive the coastguards, who were living in Littlestreet (customhaus). The second commander of the island Koch was forced, to stop the long distant patrols who controlles the streets by day and night in order to burn the beasts which has been killed from the English commando of Guernsney, to prevent epidemics on this way.

By this occation must have break up the discipline of the soldier and it has come to plunderings committed through German troops. When the on or other reader should see the pikture from what has happened twenty years ago, so he will find out I myself staying in the convent within the devastation (the picture is in possession from Mr. Bemfield, Alderney Littlestreet).

In Grand Hotel lived workmen of Guersney, I suppose 10-12 people but I am unknown because of their task. According declarations of the pilot Pope, this men took part in the devastations. I remember the fact I didn't like one person, this was Mr. Hutceson. In my office, Victoriastreet, Lloyds Bank, as no roll about people staying in Alderney.

The worksmen of Guersney have had a chairman if their own Mr. Hutceson. Certainly I met them during the time I stayed at the island (till April 1942), but it is not just present to my mind, whether I talked to him very much. Usually he sent one of his persons to me with whom I stepped to him.

---

[1] Known to the Germans as 'Flak Farm'.

I don't remember anything of the visit at Mr. Rutter. Mr Oselton lived in his house, on time I paid a visit to him. Mr. Batchelor and Mr. Clark lived in Braye Road. I believe not miss the matter when I say, that I don't remember their faces, because I didn't nearly know them. I can't say where they lived from. But certainly they could give informations to the States of Alderney about the time before I came to the island if they are living jet. Should it not be possible in that case, that the acts of the courthouse at the island Guersney are in a depot in a place of safety? when it has been so, I think, the States of Guersney would have sent back the acts after the end of the hostilities.

If one of the Misters of the States of Alderney would undertake the trouble and they should like to lay before the Misters of Guersney this matter, may be, it turns to advantage.

The first time I got the letter from the States of Alderney, this thought rised up, to examine all the workmen who have worked by that time at Alderney as far as they are attainable, naturally outside the course of law. When a court of justice will summon this people, they

Sgt. Oeser outside FK 515 HQ at Lloyds Bank, June 1941

are saying "we don't know anything about, it has been too long ago to remember this".

Now it is coming into my mind, when I, the former commissionar of Alderney, could speak to this people today, I imagine I get the one or other thing, although I am no criminal.

Likewise it may be, an ingenious hand has wall up acts in the church of St. Anne or the old tower – questions which keep me busy very much.

I have always lingered to deliver the report I wrote 10,2,42 to the States of Alderney, and according to my report from 13,3,61 has been the letter from 8.3. such an encouragement to me, that I must do it now. I know this statements contains bitternisses, but truth can't kept secret.

When I now this letter (copied and translated in English) put in Your hands, I beg you to consider always thereby, that it has been me who have done wrong in their way of acting – men as you and I – and we will not give an opinion upon this people, in order not to sin against them. You may show mercy and don't be angry with them.

This is my request by handing over my report.
Hans Herzog.

Germans herd their sheep near the airport, 1942

Herzog and Lt. Heinriche Berheim-Erft in the garden at Lloyds Bank on 10 May 1942, Herzog's last day in Alderney

Accompanying this letter, and dated 16.10.62, was a 'translation of some words' – explanations of German service terms used in the 1942 report – which was also signed by Herzog.

A reinforced company of 277 Grenadier (Infantry) Regt., under a new commandant, Capt. Carl Hoffmann, arrived in the island on 27 July 1941. Hoffmann set up his headquarters in the Drewitt's house (Seymour House), in Connaught Square, later to become the Royal Connaught Hotel. He had his officers' mess in Val des Portes. At the time of the evacuation this residence was divided into three flats and occupied by Batchelor and Clark. It was later to become the German HQ. For many years now Val des Portes has been the private residence of the Kay-Mouat family, Jon Kay-Mouat being the current (1993) president of the States of Alderney.

A secret document prepared in November 1941 by the Channel Islands Refugee Committee in London, from information smuggled out of Jersey, notes that, 'Two hundred Guernsey workmen have gone to Alderney to grow wheat'.

Up to this time the defences constructed in the island had mostly been small anti-aircraft batteries to deal with air attacks, well-placed scattered strong points,

FK 515 Alderney, staff outside Lloyds Bank, July 1941

and machine-gun posts to guard against landings on the beaches. Thousands of mines had been laid on beaches and cliffs, and barbed wire was everywhere. Most of the beaches had a clear area marked out, free of mines, for access, and agricultural land was similarly accessible. The garrison was still quite small, and many of the construction workers were paid 'volunteers'.

Things were to change drastically on 20 October 1941, when Hitler issued his top secret *Orders for the Fortification and Defence of the British Channel Islands.* There were two originals, from which ten copies were made. Although marked 'to be burned' a copy did survive, a photocopy of which is now in the Priaulx Library, Guernsey. Another photocopy, and its translation, is in Alderney museum. Hitler's orders amounted to an eight year plan to turn the Channel Islands into an impregnable fortress, the progress of which was to be reported to him, on the first of each month, via High Command. It is worth noting that, by 1944, there were almost identical numbers of heavy batteries and strong points in the islands as there were along the entire remainder of the Atlantic Wall from Dieppe to St Nazaire. By May 1945 at the German surrender, the total garrison in the islands amounted to 35,000 men.

The carrying out of this instruction required huge numbers of workers and vast amounts of concrete, and the heaviest concentration of all of this was built in little Alderney.

CHAPTER EIGHT

Silence Descends

When Hitler's orders for the intensive fortifications of the islands were issued in late 1941, normal, modest defence installations and camp accommodation had already been built, and some of the Victorian forts had been occupied, by a garrison now numbering about 450 men.

Most of what we know about the subsequent work has come firstly from the interrogation of Germans and their prisoners still in the island when it was freed, from the solid concrete evidence confronting the relieving forces, which was carefully assessed and compared with aerial photographs taken by the RAF at frequent intervals throughout the occupation, and from German documents captured at this time. Much of this material was put into official reports, a number of which appear to have been suppressed at the time or which, by some mysterious means, came to be destroyed 'to make room for later documents' before their contents were ever made public.

Since the war a number of personal diaries kept by German officers and men have been published, as well as books by British officers involved in the closing days of the war in Europe. A number of memoirs of former prisoners have also appeared in print. In more recent times various wartime letters and photographs have been found, in Alderney and elsewhere, and a number of the survivors of the slave camps, from various European countries and Russia, have given talks and newspaper interviews detailing their experiences. The work of the Channel Islands Occupation Society has unearthed more material from various official archives in Germany, England, Israel and America, as well as in the islands themselves.

Gerhard Nebel, in his book *Bei den Nordlichen Hesperiden – Tagebuch aus dem Jahre 1942* (In the Northern Hesperides – Diary of the Year 1942), gives many long entries from his diary kept at the time, and with quite lyrical descriptions of some of Alderney's natural beauties. He was a well-travelled author, not in favour with the German authorities because of his political views, and was sent to Alderney as a private soldier in a punishment company to construct fortifications. He was stationed in Alderney for five months from 24 March 1942, and was quartered in Türkenburg (Fort Tourgis). However, he spent part of the period from 11 April to 6 May in Jersey and France. Alderney was a place

SS *Irene* at the jetty waiting to take troops on leave, Easter 1942

ill-favoured by the German troops, and postings there were noted both by Nebel, and later by Baron von und zu Aufsess when he was in Guernsey in 1944, as either punishment or exile. Less polite references from the troops quartered here call Alderney '*das Arschloch der Welt*' – 'the arsehole of the world'.

Nebel shared his labour with *Organisation Todt* workers, French, Berbers, Spanish Republicans and Russian civilians. To quote his own words:

. . . . light railways, engines and lorries, all swarming with French, Algerians and Red Spaniards, which last had been interned in France.

Brief extracts from his diary show that the house on Burhou was shelled as target practice on 30 March 1942:

The German troops' canteen at Newtown, 1942. Note the mural on the gable

In front of the Fort stretches the long island of Burhou, the single house on it is today the target of the artillery for practice. It is called the Wedding Island and the story is that young newly-weds from Alderney used to spend their honeymoon there in solitude.

On 8 April Nebel was involved in overseeing the installation of an AA Battery in the eastern part of the island, and grumbled about the constant cold winds:

I always liked wind and storm. But there is so much of it and constant lack of peace makes everything an effort.

Immediately after his return from Jersey, he registered a complaint about short rations of mouldy bread, repeated at a later date, and said the soldiers were starving. His group's weapons were old captured French rifles and heavy machine-guns, and night alarms were frequent. He noted that his group erected one of the wooden camp huts in three hours. 'Much easier than working with stone', he commented. In typical army fashion he contrived to 'skive-off' and avoid as many unpleasant duties as possible:

> Albin has got a soft job and I go off to join him by using underground passages to avoid the notice of the Sgt.-Maj. We pass the time drinking and playing chess.

On 31 May Nebel went ormering, and a week or so later got punished for going without permission. He noted that cattle imported from Normandy were grazing around Burg Essex (Fort Essex). On 20 June he was drinking in St Anne with a friend, a sergeant just come from Russia who told him frightening tales of the war there, about which he commented, '. . . made my hair stand on end. Germans will have to pay bitterly for what they have done in Russia'. An interesting comment, coming as it did in 1942, which would seem to assume that Germany would eventually be defeated.

On 21 June, after drinking at the *Soldatenheim* (the convent, then a soldiers' home run by a German matron, Red Cross Sister Maria), he visited a house in town, 'probably formerly that of a doctor who had been to Oxford'. Here he found soldiers using rare and well-bound books as fuel for the cooking stove. He managed to bring away a number, including Gibbon's *Decline and Fall*, works by Bacon and Addison, Lamb and Brontë, *The Confessions of an Opium Eater*, and *The Rubaiyat of Omar Khayam*.

Nebel's duties seem to have alternated between guard and watch duties and construction of small gun emplacements. At Rose Farm, while working on the construction of defensive positions, he notes:

> . . . . potatoes and wheatfields and cattle . . . . made us self-supporting as far as possible. One hoped that at the invasion, the English would spare their own island from bombs and shells.

Occasional work at the harbour, and target practice on Platte Saline beach filled the remaining work hours. There was no hot water at Tourgis so the troops were occasionally marched up to Albertburg (Fort Albert) for a shower at the Schirrhof (Arsenal). On 14 July 1942, he saw two French women dressed 'only in pyjamas, *Organisation Todt* workers acting as cooks and washerwomen, but with a secondary function', which he states cost much, 'but they preferred payment in cigarettes and food'. A few days later he and his squad at a Flak battery, using field-glasses, watched about 100 girls offering them 'erotic sights on the beach on a Sunday afternoon'. On 30 July a school of dolphins passed along the north coast at noon.

Target practice on Platte Saline, summer 1942

On 7 August Nebel records the arrival of Russian civilian workers, dressed in evil-smelling rags, and with wooden shoes or barefoot. They were begging for food and cigarettes. (This date corresponds almost exactly with that given by Russian prisoner Kondakov for his arrival (q.v.).) On 18 August 1942 Nebel was back in Guernsey, where he found fresh fruit and dogfish in the market:

> The green and fruitful countryside is a great contrast to the barren rocky landscape of Alderney which was being covered with more and more military works.

By this time the light defences in Alderney were almost completed and manned, and camps had been built for the workers at Platte Saline (Helgoland), and in Longis Road. Possibly this refers to Borkhum, but there was also a camp, apparently a maintenance and motor transport depot, opposite the junction of Longis Road and the road to Whitegates, where the golf clubhouse now stands.

The Casquets, summer 1941

On the night of 2/3 September 1942, the third anniversary of the start of the war, Maj. G.H. March-Phillips led a group of nine officers and two men in Operation Dryad, a raid on The Casquets. At this time the German garrison on the lighthouse numbered seven men, who were all captured and taken to England with their code books and diaries. The wireless equipment was smashed. One of the Germans was apparently wearing a hairnet in bed and the soldier who captured him was reported to have said to his officer, 'I thought it was a woman, sir'. Included in the assault party was the Swede, 2nd-Lt. Anders Lassen, who was awarded the VC, MC and 2 bars during the course of the war. The following day, supplies were taken out to The Casquets by a group including George Pope, the pilot. Commenting as they approached the rock and saw no smoke coming from the chimney 'perhaps they have all gone to England', Pope was suspected of having sent information to the raiders, and later questioned for several hours.

Less than a week later, on the night of 7/8 September, another group of five officers, under Capt. Colin Ogden Smith and with Lassen in this party too, made a raid on Burhou. The attack, code-named Operation Branford, was carried out in order to establish Burhou's military potential for an assault on Alderney, but it was found to be unoccupied and the house was destroyed.

As a sequel to The Casquets raid, the German contingent there was increased
to thirty-five men, and, in October, all of the Guernsey agricultural party was
sent back to Guernsey, their work then being taken over by slave workers. They
returned later and stayed for most of the war. From that time on, however, very
little news of the Northern Isle was to be found in the Guernsey newspapers,
except for official German orders, and nothing was heard of the former
Alderney residents who had remained in the island

The Irish quarryman Peter Doyle, nephew-in-law of the Alderney greffier,
Charles Batiste, had been in Jersey with Pope when it was occupied. As a
neutral he was not interned but got himself sent back to Alderney early in 1941
where he lived at first in 'The 1720 House', in Church Street. Later he and his
wife moved to Lloyds Bank where they acted as housekeeper and general
handyman to Herzog, and, for a time, Doyle drove the Wolseley car belonging
formerly to the National Provincial Bank and used throughout the occupation
by German officers as a staff car. A son, Eddie, was born to them during this
time.

Young Eddie Doyle, son of the Irishman Peter, who was born in Alderney during the war, in the
garden of Lloyds Bank with Herzog's dog, summer 1941

Farmer Frank Oselton was now based at Watermill Farm, which had been surrounded with barbed wire possibly to prevent theft of his livestock (fourteen cows and a bull). Assisted by Ernest Clark, Oselton existed by selling his milk to the Germans. Nebel appears to have met him earlier, on 25 July 1942, and notes that he '. . . . appeared to have got over his wife and children being in England, as he is now living with another woman'.

George Pope, an English merchant seaman, had only arrived in the island as the war started, sailing from Jersey in a small yacht with his wife, three children and mother-in-law. He had been in Jersey when Alderney was first occupied, but had persuaded the German authorities to allow him and his wife (who had been taken to Guernsey by that time) to return to the island. They lived at 4 The Val. He acted as a pilot for the German ships throughout the rest of the war. During this time the Popes had three more children, one of whom, Anthony, died in 1943 aged two years. The last of these, Elizabeth, was born on 15 May 1945, a few days before the island was freed. The family left the island soon after it was relieved in 1945, and finally settled near Newmarket. Mrs Pope eventually had fourteen children, and George Pope died in 1988.

There is also a record of Tommy Oliver, who had come back to Alderney with the first Guernsey party and was then 'custodian in charge of houses and property'. He apparently remained, living at the Albert House on the corner of Victoria Street and Ollivier Street, where he had lived before the war. Little more is known about him or the others who stayed. It is a subject that seems never to be discussed among those who returned, and by now most of them are dead.

On 14 May 1943 a group of twenty-six 'volunteer' building workers from Jersey (of whom twenty were 'conscripted') was brought to Alderney in SS *Irene*, travelling over two nights via Guernsey. Their 'call-up' papers were issued by FK 515, and guaranteed that:

> Service of labour is not demanded for work of any kind which would imply active participation in active warfare against your own country. The right to give notice is suspended until further notice.

They were employed by the *Wehrmacht Heeresunterkunftsverwaltung 130*, (*HUV* – Army Billeting Office), and not by OT, and were to be paid 84 pfennig an hour. They expected to be in the island for six months, and were billeted in the Jubilee Home in High Street, the former almshouse.

There were already a few Guernseymen, with their own cook, billeted in the Victoria Hotel, and they were moved in with the Jersey group. The jobs they were given included roofing the new bakehouse in Le Vallée, building an office

Watermill Farm shadowed by Fort Tourgis, 1941

for *HUV* in Ollivier Street, repairing the roof of the stone-crusher, and repairing the French-made bunk-beds used by the army. Shortly after their arrival, six Jersey lorry drivers were brought over to work in the docks transporting food, and carrying water from the battery quarry to the various outlying units. One Jerseyman was apparently operating the power station.

Working hours for the party were 8 a.m.–12 noon and 2 p.m.–6 p.m., with a half-day on Saturday, and Sundays free. Food was adequate but not plentiful. They were told they received the same rations as the troops, but doubted if that were so. One of the party recently remembered (1992) that the daily rations were ¼ of a loaf of bread plus butter, which had to be divided between morning and evening with the substitute coffee issued, and at midday, meat and vegetables prepared by the Guernsey cook, sometimes with soup as well. They occasionally managed to obtain extra food from another Guernseyman employed as a cook at the *Soldatenheim* by sneaking in through the back door. They also collected winkles from Braye beach and cooked them in their rooms.

The German *HUV* staff consisted of *Oberzahlmeister* Lenz, later replaced by *Oberzahlmeister* Lamm, 3 NCOs, 1 clerk, and 3 or 4 Ukrainians from Helgoland camp who returned there each evening.

Cpl. Müller and lobster pot on Longis Beach

The workers were allowed to write home once a month. Mail was handed to the *HUV* office in Alderney, and arrived in Jersey with Guernsey 2½d. stamps on the envelopes, and civilian postmarks. Return mail was simply addressed to the man at '*HUV* Alderney, CI', and carried Jersey 2½d. stamps and, again, no military marks.

All the men were returned to Jersey in October 1943, in small parties travelling at night on a small coaster to Cherbourg, then by train to St Malo, where they all collected together and were shipped back to Jersey.

At the time of its relief, there was, of course, a very considerable investigation into the occupation happenings in Alderney. Maj. T.X.H. Pantcheff, an intelligence officer, whose uncle, Dr Ramsbotham, was one of the three doctors in Alderney at the time of the evacuation, interviewed most of the 1,000 or so persons still on the island at the time, including all of the remaining Germans and most of the foreign workers. As a result of his investigations, he later spent two years tracing Max List, the commandant of Sylt, but found only the false evidence of his death in Italy.

One curious phenomenon noted by a number of the slaves who were brought to the island later in the war, as well as by some of the returning inhabitants afterwards, was the silence. It seems that few birds sang in Alderney during the war, and they did not return in any numbers for a further five years after the war.

Whether this is really so or not, it is the material from which legends arise. One thing is certain, however. Before the war there was no gannet colony here. After the return of the islanders, at the beginning of 1946, small numbers of the birds were noted both on Ortac and Les Guardiens (The Garden Rocks or Les Étacs), and these quickly built up to form substantial colonies which still arrive annually in late January or early February and depart in October. It is thought that they may have moved from Lundy Island in the Bristol Channel, a former colony used as a bombing range during the war. The Germans made no record of either colony as far as we can find, and the second edition (1944) of their island guide, which has sections on the flora and fauna, makes no mention of these birds.

CHAPTER NINE

Slave Island

The departure of the Guernsey party left Alderney totally in the hands of the enemy, with virtually no-one to witness their activities, apart from the very small number of islanders and other 'British' who had remained, and who must all have worked for the occupying power in one way or another.

At this time the German Command was divided into three sections.

Civil Affairs
Under HQ 515 CA Unit in Guernsey. Responsible for the 'volunteers' and civilian workers.

Military
C.-in-C. Jersey in overall command. Alderney came under the direct control of Guernsey. Responsible for the 'Watch and Ward' function, manning trenches and forward positions, anti-aircraft defences, etc. The ack-ack unit was housed in the Grand Hotel after the Guernsey group left.

Organisation Todt
Responsible for supplying 'labour'. This at first consisted of parties of well-paid French, North African, and 'Red' Spanish workers. The French at least were allowed home leave about every three months. Dr Todt paid a visit to Alderney in November 1941, just after Hitler's 'Fortification Order' was issued.

The Channel Islands were all given code names by the Germans. Alderney was known as *Adolph*, and many of the prisoners apparently never knew it by any other name.

Capt. Hoffmann remained in the island for some time, but with the arrival of officers of superior rank became subordinate in turn to Lt.-Col. Gleden, Maj. Martin, Lt.-Col. Rohde and, in February 1942, to Maj. Zucke, who was soon promoted to Lt.-Col., and remained until November 1943. From then until the surrender, the island commandant was Lt.-Col. Schwalm, with *Hauptmann* Fricher as his adjutant.

In early 1942 the paid *Todt* workers formed the largest part of the German force. There were also a number of slaves, mostly Jews from Paris and a few German political prisoners, employed as dockers, in building the machine shops, and in making the Lower Road. They lived in the islanders' houses in a wired-off section of Newtown. The gate pillars of the entrance to this compound, which also contained the workshops and machine-shops, are still to be seen along Lower Road at the entrance to the Banquage Estate.

Hoffmann was promoted to major in July 1942 and *Bauleiter* Leo Ackermann who lived at North Star in Victoria Street was put in charge of the *Todt* workers. The official designation of this unit was the Firma Ackermann, as shown on a document preserved in the museum. His position was that of construction superintendent, and his rank equivalent to major. He received masses of cement and slave labourers, principally Russian civilians.

The camp *Lager Norderney* had been built in January 1941, with wooden sectional huts brought directly from the firm of De Cuhn in Belgium, and with Belgian workers to erect them. It was near the lighthouse, on the site of the present-day States camping ground, and with an old railway bridge giving direct access to Arch Bay through its tunnel. Later stories about the prisoners being threatened with imprisonment and, consequently, suffocation in this tunnel as doors and vents were sealed, are not borne out, as examination of the tunnel reveals no trace of hinges on which doors could have been hung. Gordon Prigent, a Jerseyman sent to Alderney as a punishment, explained that there was a brick wall with a gate inside the tunnel (the wall can still be seen about half-way along the tunnel), and they were to be herded in there with a machine-gun trained on them, to be shot if Allied troops made a landing.

Shortly after Norderney was finished a group of French women were brought in as 'cooks'. The first job of the *Todt* workers in this camp was to start the construction of the anti-tank wall at Longis Bay.

In November 1941 a Spitfire, piloted by Flying Officer Greenaway, was shot down by a Messerschmitt 109, and made a crash landing on Longis Beach, an incident witnessed by Helmut Asbeck, who was fishing for lobsters nearby. To the amazement of the Germans working there, the pilot stepped virtually unhurt from the crashed aircraft. He was housed in the Belle Vue Hotel for a few days before being taken to Guernsey. In the dogfight in which he was involved he had already shot down another ME 109. Five days earlier another Spitfire from his 'wing', piloted by American Flying Officer Myers, had been shot down by AA fire over Alderney, and crash-landed at Braye.

In addition to *Lager Helgoland*, near Fort Tourgis, and *Lager Norderney*, each capable of holding 1,500 prisoners, there was also *Lager Borkhum*, similar in size and situated just off the Longis Road, and *Lager Sylt*, just west of Val L'Emauve

Helmut Asbeck 'looking out for the RAF'

Going lobster fishing in Longis Bay, August 1941

near the airport. *Lager Borkhum* was largely used to house the German technicians, and skilled OT workers, members of various OT 'firms', who were brought in from various countries at different times for specific tasks, and as such was perhaps not truly a slave camp.

There was also a small reception camp, *Lager Citadella*. Identified by the International Red Cross, its position was not positively confirmed, but was either at Newtown, or more likely near the present States dairy in Le Val, then newly built by the Germans as a field butchery.

These camps were all quickly erected using sectional buildings shipped from Cherbourg. From this time there were at least 2,500–3,000 slave workers available, and German records found in Jersey show the peak at about 4,000 in May 1943. However, one Red Cross investigator, Alfred Herzka, in a lecture given in Alderney in 1970, put the number as high as 7,000 at its peak.

The slave workers were expected to work at least twelve hours a day, seven days a week, on very little food. The prisoner's rations, as mentioned by several different writers who all agree closely, were:

Breakfast – ½ litre of ersatz coffee;
Lunch – ½ litre of thin cabbage soup, taken in a short break at the work site;
Supper – as for lunch but with the addition of a 1 kg loaf, to be shared between five or six men.

The inner gate pillars of Sylt camp, photographed in 1989

There was never any milk, sugar or meat, and if they took the rest day allowed every week or occasionally two weeks, they were not fed on that day. The principal applied was *Nicht arbeit, nicht essen* – if you don't work, you don't eat.

Prisoners claimed that the officers were selling their food to the French and Algerian whores for gold, and that the guards were sending it to Guernsey, where a considerable 'black market' existed.

The workers were arranged in 'castes', and the Vichy French were treated well and got their paid leave every three or four months. Helgoland camp on Platte Saline was principally used for the Russian and Ukranian civilians, Norderney for civilians of other nationalities – Belgians, Poles, Czechs, Spaniards, and apparently two Chinese, one of whom, Ki-Lieng Tien, was later beaten to death by an SS guard, *Unterlagerführer* Heinrich Evers. His body was taken to Guernsey and buried in the Foulon Cemetery.

As we have seen, Borkhum at first housed the German specialist workers, and Citadella the Moroccan POWs, who were later transferred to a camp near the newly-built German bakery in Le Vallée.

Sylt, which is clearly shown at an early stage of building on an aerial photograph dated 30.9.1942, was set up for 500 political prisoners who had to

Borkhum camp from the air, 12 June 1944

build it themselves. It was under Hoffmann's control for a few weeks, until, in late March 1943, it was taken over by the SS *Totenkopfverband* (Death's-Head Brigade). Under SS *Sturmbaunführer* Maximilian List, an SS member since 1930, the brigade comprised thirteen officers and forty-seven guards. Sylt was then filled with 1,000 political prisoners brought from Neuengamme camp, and about 120 German *Wehrmacht* officers accused of treason, a group said to have included three generals whom it would have been politically unwise for Hitler to have shot. These officers were distinguished by an upside-down red triangle, sewn on the sleeve of their blue and white striped concentration camp 'pyjamas', which were not apparently worn by the other prisoners in Alderney. It became the only concentration camp ever built on British soil.

By mid-June 1943 about 300 of the Sylt prisoners are said by Steckoll to have died, and during the next week fifty more died. Some doubt has been cast on the credibility of Steckoll's information, but in the summer of 1982, and even later in 1985, Herr Otto Spehr, former prisoner number 17147 in Sylt camp, returned to Alderney and imparted details of his researches after the war to former intelligence officer, Maj. T.X.H. Pantcheff, an Alderney resident until his death in 1989. Spehr had returned to Neuengamme near Hamburg shortly after the war, and photographed all the master records of deaths in the camp from March 1943 to February 1944, the last three and a half months of the camp's existence being unrecorded. These put the deaths in a somewhat different light from the previous official British records, as will be seen later.

List and his assistant, SS *Obersturmführer* Kurt Klebeck, responsible for security, were taken to Berlin in the autumn of 1943 and tried for allowing prisoners to escape. The prisoners in question were part of a consignment of 200, too weak to work, who were being shipped from Sylt supposedly to the gas chambers at Neuengamme. Some managed to break their way out of the train after leaving Cherbourg. List and Klebeck were acquitted and returned to Alderney, and the records of this trial remain some of the few kept by the Germans that authenticate the very existence of this concentration camp. These German records confirm that prisoners too ill or too weak to work were removed from the island to another fate.

Herr Spehr's researches into the official records showed that a total of eighty-seven prisoners at Sylt died during the spring and summer of 1943, sixty-five of whom had been identified as being buried in the Russian graves at Longis. These were mainly Russian and Ukrainian prisoners of war. Of the others, fifteen were Poles and seven Germans.

Herr Spehr has testified that he saw thirty-nine prisoners killed in mid-April 1943, and another group in February 1944. They were all too weak to continue working and were driven out of the camp gates and then shot, 'trying to escape'.

In the Neuengamme records the names of the first group were spread out over two months, the second group over several days, but not all of the names appeared in that list. Herr Spehr also identified two prisoners hanged on the orders of SS *Obersturmführer* Klebeck. His later researches were reported in 1985, and by this time he had turned up records of a statement made by SS *Hauptscharführer* Otto Högelow, the warrant-officer in charge of the guards at Sylt, to the Austrian Criminal Police in May 1945. Högelow had been commander of the camp guard unit before it left Dusseldorf *en route* for Alderney, and had killed two prisoners and wounded a third during this time. Sixty men escaped, of whom six were recaptured and killed. After arriving in Alderney he and a number of other German guards and some of the 'habitual criminal' prisoners were responsible for many more deaths. Some dozen of these were named in his statement.

After the Allied invasion of Europe, Högelow threatened all of the German prisoners that they would be killed before anything could happen to the guards. Any guard who killed an escaping prisoner would be given three days' special

VP 703 was wrecked in Braye Bay while attempting to tow the *Xaver Dorsch* to safety during a storm

leave and twenty-five cigarettes. The prisoners were removed from Alderney
shortly after, and thirty-three were shot during the train journey between 24
June and 1 August 1944. Twenty prisoners were shot after four escaped between
Tours and the Belgian border. They finally arrived at a camp in Solletedt in
Saxony (central Germany), which came under the administration of
Buchenwald. In December 1944 they were transferred to Sachsenhausen
concentration camp, but in April 1945 were again moved, first to Berlin, and
then into Bohemia. On the way 168 escaped, and many more were shot, after
the train had been attacked by Allied fighter-bombers. The American forces
eventually liberated the few surviving captives in May 1945.

In January 1943, the 515 ton MV *Xaver Dorsch*, named after the director of the
OT in Berlin, broke loose from her moorings at No. 3 berth in a violent storm.
On board were 300 Russian prisoners who were too weak to be of further use and
so were being shipped back to Europe. The *Xaver Dorsch* was stranded on the rocks
in the middle of the bay. Some of the prisoners had already died from being
crammed in below decks while waiting for the ship to sail, and more lost their lives
in the wreck. Little is known about this vessel, although she may have been
refloated as another source reported her sunk by Allied aircraft off Lezardrieux on

The wrecks of *VP 703* (left) and MV *Henny Fricke* in Braye Bay, 1945

29 April 1944. There are, however, some remains of three ships still at this site: SS *Burton*, wrecked in 1911; *VP 703*; and, probably, the *Henny Fricke*, wrecked here in 1943. At very low tides the boilers and keels of two, and the bow section of *VP 703* may still be seen. Helmut Lücke, a seaman in the Harbour Guard at the time, recently visited Alderney (1990) and brought with him some photographs taken at the time of the storm. One of the pictures shows what appears to be *Xaver Dorsch* still attached by a tow line to the *VP 703*, which had attempted to tow it off and was itself wrecked in the process.

However little sense it would appear to make now, there can be little doubt that hard manual labour was expected from men given the barest subsistence level of food, and that they were replaced when their usefulness had passed, despite the extra difficulty of transporting them to and from mainland Europe.

Sylt continued to exist for seventeen months until it was evacuated, and all except one hut destroyed, in July 1944. By then, it was estimated that only about 500 prisoners, including most of the *Wehrmacht* officers, still survived.

One of the unique fire-proof sentry boxes guarding Sylt camp

By a curious 'coincidence', the one remaining hut was totally destroyed by fire on the eve of Yom Kippur in October 1970. All that remains of the camp today are the gateposts, some concrete hut bases, and two unique circular, fireproof, concrete sentry boxes.

The commandant, Max List, had had a bungalow built for himself just outside the camp, in a fine sheltered spot, looking out to sea down the Val L'Emauve, and connected by a tunnel to the camp bath-house. After the war this bungalow was taken down and re-erected on a site on Longis Common, completed by the addition of two wings and a swimming pool, and today forming an elegant, shingle hung, cedar-wood home. The terrace on which it was originally built, with the drain connections and the tunnel, is still there and is easily reached from the rough south coast road.

When Sylt was evacuated, List was transferred to Oslo in Norway, then to Italy, and later to Berlin, where he faked his own death, apparently in Italy in 1945, and escaped retribution. He was reputedly still alive in West Germany in 1982.

By early 1943 the defences on the island were well advanced, and troops occupied all of the forts, except possibly Les Hommeaux Florains and Houmet

Sylt camp from the air. Note the trenches running across the airfield site

The Commandant's tunnel, taken in 1989

The former house of the Commandant, taken in 1989. The house is now situated on Longis Common

Herbé. In all, according to German records, 30,317 mines had been laid, barbed wire was everywhere, there was an extensive network of underground concrete emplacements, ammunition stores and shelters, and several underground storage tunnels, one of the largest, under Essex Hill, over 200 yd long and about 15 ft across. A number of heavy guns were in place and operational, and the command post at Mannez was constructed.

In November 1943, Maj. Carl Hoffmann was transferred to Jersey where he remained until the surrender in May 1945. According to British official records, he was said to have been extradited to Russia, and hanged in public in the square at Kiev in autumn 1945. More recent research by Solomon Steckoll, published in *The Alderney Death Camp* in 1982, suggests that he remained in a British POW camp until 1948 when he was released. He then returned to West Germany, where he died on 8 March 1974.

Although time may have dimmed their memory a little, and the horrors they saw and endured will no doubt have coloured their viewpoint, the various personal memoirs, books, letters, talks and interviews given and written by former slaves can by no means be discounted. Some of the difficulties encountered in finding official documents makes one wonder about the accuracy of the official figures for the numbers of slaves who both worked and died in Alderney during its occupation. Steckoll, for example, a South-African born, Israeli journalist who spent two years researching his book, found that many documents, particularly Russian, were 'not available', and that some British ones had been apparently destroyed for 'lack of space'. There also appear to have been frequent transfers of groups of workers to and from Europe, which may affect the accuracy of any records.

Even Charles Cruikshank, who was given every possible facility for the production of the official history *The German Occupation of the Channel Islands*, published in 1975, had cause to comment on the unsatisfactory handling of the demilitarization and evacuation from the Channel Islands, and the apparent indifference to the fate of the islanders shown by the British Government in the last months of the war in Europe.

Suggestions have been made that Clement Attlee, Prime Minister of the first British post-war government, had evidence of collaboration and 'war crimes' by Channel Islanders suppressed, so that there would be 'no record of British subjects behaving incorrectly'. Winston Churchill was reported to have cancelled a planned visit to the islands shortly after their liberation when stories reached him of the number of German-fathered babies born to island girls, known locally as 'Jerry-bags' in Jersey and Guernsey. It is also possible that it was not wished to upset or alarm the returning islanders by stories of atrocities or excessive violence occurring in their homelands and especially in evacuated Alderney.

The entrance to the German tunnel under Essex Hill, 1989

One of several junctions in the tunnel on the south side of Water Lanes. Note the turntable for the narrow gauge railway

If one considers the extreme conditions under which thousands of slaves worked in the islands, particularly in Alderney, the frequent beatings, and the poor rations they had to survive on, about which there is general agreement, it would be strange indeed if the recorded figures of only 335 deaths in Alderney (plus or minus ten), carefully extracted from official German documents, truly represent all who died here. It also seems certain that several batches of prisoners, too weak or sick to be of further use as workers, were taken back to the mainland of Europe, and that many of these died or were killed *en route* for their final destination.

There is evidence to suggest that at least some of the sick prisoners, sent back to mainland Europe from the islands, were given any necessary hospital treatment, and were well fed and rested before being put to work again.

Whatever the truth, some Channel Island people, who might have been thought by their fellow islanders to have co-operated rather too closely and willingly with the German authorities, were given honours after the war which effectively stopped any action being taken against them. None of the few islanders or British subjects who remained on Alderney were ever tried or punished.

There is only a little evidence to suggest that German officers and men, or 'trusty' prisoners, the 'kapos', were tried for their crimes. Seven SS officers and one 'kapo', Gustav Adolf Fehrenbacher, were tried for murder and mass murder of prisoners, both in Alderney and during their evacuation from the island after D-Day. Although later released under amnesty, the accused were sentenced to four years' imprisonment. One, Sgt.-Maj. Högelow, died in 1983 at Pinneberg in Holstein, Germany.

These must surely represent a very small portion of those culpable in this respect.

However, the purpose here is not to pass judgement on these matters, and, indeed, long-time island resident T.X.H. Pantcheff, the intelligence officer on the spot shortly after Alderney was relieved, firmly refuted any suggestion of a official British 'cover-up' in his *Alderney – Fortress Island*, published in 1981, an opinion only slightly modified by later evidence which he received. It seems fair, nonetheless, to present the slaves' side of the story as well, as told in various publications and communications.

Sadly, Maj. T.X.H. 'Bunny' Pantcheff died in Alderney, at the age of 69, while the manuscript of this book was being prepared and some time before the release of the official documents. The benefit of his comments and advice has been sadly missed.

Carbon copies of MI9 documents came into the possession of the *Mail on Sunday* newspaper in the summer of 1992 and extracts were published on

2 August. Several of these were statements made by German soldiers and former prisoners, Russian, Spanish and British, to the investigating officer shortly after Alderney was relieved. These all tend to confirm that beatings and torture were commonplace, not only by the SS but also by OT officials, and that the total number of deaths was far higher than the official figures published at the time. It seems unlikely that the true figure will ever be known.

On 1 December 1992, under pressure created by several MPs, including David Winnick, the British Government decided to release much of the documentation about the occupation of the Channel Islands previously held under a 100 year embargo. Claims were made in newspapers that the papers show there to have been a considerable amount of co-operation between the island authorities in Jersey and Guernsey and the occupying power.

As far as Alderney is concerned, however, there were only the handful of civilians who remained, none of whom had held any official positions, and only three being Alderneymen. These claims were immediately refuted by Guernsey's Bailiff, Graham Dorey, based on the evidence of the 2,400 files relating to the administration of the island during the occupation which include the complete minutes of the Controlling Committee meetings and those of the German civil administration. The committee was often able to delay the carrying out of peremptory German orders, and occasionally ignored them altogether, despite the threat of action against the civilian population which resulted in the deportation of several to Germany, including the *Procureur du Roi*, Ambrose Sherwill.

Subsequent to the release of the PRO records, these closed files in the Guernsey Greffe were opened to public scrutiny on 5 January 1993. Little confirmation of official co-operation in Guernsey was found, except for the references to persons informing on the presence of the five women of Jewish extraction in the island, who were subsequently deported to Germany. Three of them, all of German origin, later died in Auschwitz. The proclamations and events leading to their deportation were, in any case, fully reported in the newspapers at the time. As was already well known, paid volunteer workers also went to Alderney from both Jersey and Guernsey at various times, usually for specific jobs which they were assured were not connected with military operations. All of the Guernsey files had been available to Charles Cruikshank when he wrote the official history, *The German Occupation of the Channel Islands*, published in 1975.

Records for deaths of slave workers in Alderney detail, for instance, twenty-three deaths in Norderney camp in one month in October 1942. This figure is similar to the figures given by one prisoner, mentioned in the *Mail on Sunday* article, that 73 Russians, 2 Frenchmen and 1 woman died there in a three month period from July 1943. The German death certificates are all signed by a doctor, carry the official OT stamp and give the cause of death, mostly from dysentery, enteritis, hepatitis, septicaemia and gangrene.

Kurt Klebeck, deputy commandant of Sylt camp for about a year, had been found by investigators in May 1992 to be still alive in Hamburg. Now aged 86, and after denying ever being in Alderney in previous interviews, he finally admitted to having been in Alderney in a telephone interview broadcast by Radio Guernsey on 17 January 1993. He referred the interviewer to his lawyer and broke the connection when questioned about his activities here. When contacted, his lawyer stated that his client was unaware of any crimes during his time in Alderney and had not been involved in any.

In the same broadcast, Ted Mesovicz, a Pole who had been a slave worker at Sylt camp at the age of 16, claimed to have seen men shot, tortured and beaten to death. He also mentioned a team of eighty prisoners being made to work non-stop for two days and nights pouring concrete for a bunker in torrential rain and wind. This story was ratified by former Russian prisoner Georgi Kondakov, also 16 at the time, and is noted in the next chapter.

The Home Office adviser on war crimes, Dr Anthony Glees, also stated in the broadcast that:

> We know that at least 16,000 slave-labourers were kept in four concentration camps on Alderney and that it was deliberate German SS policy to work slave labourers to death. . . . I should be surprised if the numbers killed by the Nazis did not run into thousands and not just tens and hundreds.

Only Sylt camp was actually a concentration camp run by the SS and the general consensus is that there were never more than 5,000 slave workers in the island at any one time. This figure can therefore be presumed to refer to the total number brought to the island during the whole occupation period, and will also include all of those taken back to France at various times for whatever reason or purpose, as well as those who were still in the island at the liberation and those who died from all causes.

CHAPTER TEN

Prisoner in Alderney

'Island of Death in the Channel' – thus reads the heading of an article written by journalist Galina Chernakova, published in the Russian young people's newspaper *Komsomolskaya Pravda* on 8 May 1989.

The article resulted from a letter to *Pravda* from a former slave of the Germans in Alderney, living in the town of Orel, south-west of Moscow, which was followed up by an invitation from the author's wife, the honorary curator of the Alderney museum, to three other Russian journalists, who visited Alderney the week before this article was published.

The article has been translated by Royston Raymond, teacher of French at the Alderney public school.

'Dear Editor,
I write to you as a former prisoner of the Fascist prison camp Heligoland, situated during the war on the British Island of Alderney.'

Thus starts a letter which came to the Editor from G.I. Kondakov in Orel. It must be admitted that, until now, it had never come to my notice that in 1940 the British Channel Islands were occupied, and that on two tiny plots of dry land, Alderney and Jersey, the Hitlerite forces built camps to which thousands of Soviet citizens were sent.

I decided to go to Orel to the writer of that letter in order to learn further details. It turned out that Georgi Ivanovitch, one of 93 former prisoners in Alderney (still alive), wrote down from memory everything that had happened to him during those dreadful years.

Obviously G.I. Kondakov is not an historian and perhaps in his account there are some inexact details, for the human memory is not a document. That, however, in my opinion is not important, the main thing is that the reminiscences of this man have a trueness-to-life. He has seen with his own eyes and experienced in himself the fate of a slave of the Third Reich, and had the ability not only to survive inhuman conditions, but to stand up to them and conquer them.

Former Russian slaves in 1983. Kondakov is standing fourth from the left

It is really not only curiosity which makes us want to know these things. Without them it is not possible to understand what Fascism is, and how to stand up against it. Without them it is impossible to determine one's own attitude to people who have themselves experienced the workings of the Fascist machine of destruction of men and humanity.

Today we publish extracts from the memoirs of G.I. Kondakov.

The extract from Mr Kondakov's memoirs then begins.

The Germans came to Orel completely unexpectedly. No-one gave us warning. In the 'Medredeva' factory where all we apprentices were stationed just after the beginning of the war, work was in full swing. Suddenly explosions and shots were heard. Fires started. I and Vasey Mosicheff, friends since Technical College, rushed outside into the street and were stunned – we saw three tanks with Swastikas on them firing at the factory. What was to become of us? We decided each to go to his own home. That's how we separated and we did not meet again until 1942 in Frankfurt-am-Maine.

In May 1942, in Mertzalovka (25 km from Orel), a German rearguard unit established itself. The Fascists were setting up their 'New Order'. The land was shared among the peasants like under the Tsars, and they apppointed a controller – a *Burgomeister*. This was a former primary school head, Ivan Kirikovitch (I don't remember his surname exactly – it was something like Pshkoff). He told, or rather gave, evidence to the Germans that his father was a White officer. As proof of his trustworthiness he denounced his wife Yergenia Ivanovna, a teacher of Russian Language and Literature. She was a member of the 'party' and the Germans shot her.

Soon there came the order to send labour forces to Germany. In Mertzalovka they took a pair of both sexes from large families. The controller would approach the father and say, 'Ivan, you have 5 children, – what about giving up some of them?", as though he were talking of a pair of boots, not people. To struggle was useless, the Germans strictly disciplined you. There was no escaping or getting out of it. They shot one whole family.

In Frankfurt-am-Maine was a sort of assembly and dispersal point for labour forces. We arrived at night and at first were herded into a barracks. The dawn made visible a thousand little notes in Russian, Ukrainian, White Russian and Polish which entirely covered the walls and even the ceiling. To this day I can remember how the words pierced my heart – scratched in pencil by some unknown Oxana from Poltovshchina, 'Tell my dear mother that I will never forget her or my little brothers'.

At 6 a.m. a gong sounded and they herded us out onto the square and sorted us into groups: young men, women, and old men. They ordered those who had some sort of special skills to step forward – for work in German factories. A few men stepped forward, then an officer in a black uniform, who until now had been standing like a statue, barked curtly and pointed with his whip to a barrack nearby. I glanced that way and gasped. Behind the windows that were covered with thick, rusty barbed-wire stood living skeletons. They stretched out their thin, stick-like arms and softly begged, 'Brothers, give us a little bread'. It appeared that they were fellow countymen of ours who had been working in the mines in Belgium. 'Now they have only one journey to make – to the crematorium!', shouted an interpreter. 'Those who hide their special skills must expect the same fate.'

I must admit that then I had not heard tell of such crematoria, but even so the picture presented to me stunned me. A few more men took a step

OT workers digging a trench, 1942

forward. Among them was a fellow villager from Novoloonige, Nicholas Anokhih . . . , but among my fellow apprentices standing in the same rank as I, no-one stood forward.

Then once again it was the boarded-up goods waggon, the monotonous rattle of the wheels, the heat, and the thirst that grabbed you by the throat.

From Frankfurt-am-Maine we went to Brussels, and from Brussels to the French town of St Malo – right on the coast. From there was one more step to the tiny island occupying barely 8 sq kms of dry land, which was fated to play such an evil part in my life.

The boat moved alongside the jetty in Alderney at dawn on 8 August 1942, about 4 a.m. (I don't remember the date myself, but depend on my friend's advice.) We were transported along a broken road leading from the harbour. Around us were scattered what looked like muddy rags, the local inhabitants had thrown away their belongings in their hurry in leaving Alderney. Then we saw grey stone houses, and above them a church with a

Slave workers with a German OT overseer behind Longis Villas, 1942

a weathercock instead of a cross. A steep turning road,[1] and there we were, in front of some gates over which there was an arch with 'Helgoland' written on it in Gothic script. This was the camp.

Beyond the barbed wire were some wooden huts set round a level square where men in light brown military uniforms were staring at us. On their sleeves we could make out red armbands with a white circle and a black swastika and the words 'Todt Organisation'. (As I learnt after the war, this organization, founded by Dr Fritz Todt in the thirties, provided various German firms with labour forces, pouring into Fascist Germany from the enslaved countries of Europe, and all over the world. The light brown clothing of the Todt members was none other than captured

---

[1]The road past the RC church at Crabby went part way up Le Vallée and round behind Picaterre Farm (Route Picaterre) and the brewery, at this time. The present straight part along from the junction with Route Picaterre to the bottom of Le Vallée was built later, by the Germans, and shows on RAF aerial photographs dated 1944, but not on earlier ones.

Czech military uniforms.) Our camp was guarded like all the camps in
Alderney, in the main by SS men. Given the number 167 I was enrolled
into the firm 'Shtrabag', which undertook the building and repair of
roads. On the very first day we were driven to work (driven on foot, by
the guards) on the other, eastern end of the island where we had to make
up the roadway to Fort Albert. Gradually the 'Deathsheads' (we
nicknamed them this from the similarity of the swastika with its crossed
bones to the skull and crossbones) began to grow violent. On the way
sticks and pick-axe handles appeared. A Pole, Stanislav, much older than
me and working right next to me explained that I must not anger the
Deathsheads, that I must pretend to get stuck in. 'Immer Arbeit' – always
work – this was the motto of the Germans. Later I learnt that Stanislav, at
the beginning of the thirties, had worked for a few years in Germany. He
had come to Alderney of his free will and not long ago he had got
married, and the young lord of the manor demanded his feudal right,
Stanislav slept on the bunk next to mine. I helped him as I could, and in
a way he helped me to survive. He, however, has remained forever on
that accursed island.

Day after day dragged past. At 6 a.m. we got up. At first the guards bang
on the wooden walls of the huts with their sticks, then they burst in and
with shouts of 'Aufstehen', they start to flog anyone who comes within
reach. There were certainly no washing facilities on the island. There was
not enough freshwater – hence during my whole fourteen months on
Alderney I never once washed. Then we were driven to the eating hall
where we were pushed in to drink so-called coffee – a black dishwater
with a disgusting smell which caused men to swell up and die.

For dinner, which lasted half an hour, they brought us 'bunkersoup' – a
watery almost flavourless gruel in which morsels of cucumber and pitiful
slices of cabbage could be distinguished. Bunkersoup was usually
distributed by a stalwart negro. He was a terrible man. He possessed a
remarkable strength and would beat people unmercifully. Before our eyes,
he killed one young fellow with one blow of his ladle, apparently for
coming up for a second helping. In the evening we would be given a
ration of 1 litre of the same gruel, and half a loaf of bread – this was
supposed to last sometimes three and at times four days.

The problem of bread was even worse in Sylt camp. There, over a long
period, the prisoners were given only one loaf a week. Starving men could
not stand this – they would gobble down their ration straight away, and
then later die of hunger. Sylt was the most dreadful place in Alderney. Out
of sixteen barrack huts only thirteen were occupied and in the remaining

huts were piled up corpses. Lorries carrying bodies surely went there. By February 1943 the camp was almost deserted, desolate.

On Alderney there were neither gas chambers nor crematoria, public executions were not carried out either. However, the very conditions of existence were such that, in my estimation, only one in five survived. I reckon that between 1942 and 1943 more than five thousand prisoners were brought to the island from the USSR and on the 14 October 1943, at the most, only 986 men were taken to France.

I can state the figures exactly, as later I worked in the assembly point for Soviet Citizens in liberated Paris, and I drew up the register myself of my former comrades from Alderney.

Certainly among the prisoners in Alderney one finds not only those who died from hunger and sickness, but from boundless greed. A few went willingly to Germany to earn easy money. These people ended up in the dreadful conditions of Alderney, where it would seem all OUR strength was concentrated on one thing – to survive – but they could not save themselves from their own craving for money grabbing. Within a few weeks of their arrival in the island they began to barter bread for other things. On the black market half a loaf could buy a tweed suit, leather boots and many other things. At the end of August the man in the bunk next to me died from hunger. When the body was taken away they found under the mattress, tightly packed in layers, three pairs of boots and six suits. How much could be said about this! However such cases were obviously isolated. In the main people just died, as you might say.

A particularly high death rate was reached towards the end of 1942. After the war A.W. Pianoff, a former prisoner in Sylt camp, can now calmly tell, 'on one occasion somehow I hurt my arm badly and was confined to camp for a few days, and had to carry away the bodies. From those three barrack sheds standing amidst the fern, we each day dragged 20–30 bodies. Transport of the bodies just couldn't be kept up with. Plump rats ran over the faces of the dead, and ate the noses, ears and lips'.

And this is how V.I. Rosslov from Helgoland camp remembers it: 'usually they didn't bury the bodies at all but just threw them in the sea. A lorry loaded with corpses would go to the very end of the breakwater, which stuck out about 500 metres into the bay, dump its horrible load, and come back'.

It is true that they stopped doing that at the end of 1942. The new 'Frontführer', Lucian Link, put in charge of Alderney by the Todt

Organisation, expressed his displeasure that, 'Russian corpses were littering the sea'. At Christmas, at morning 'coffee break', it was announced over the loudspeakers: 'Gentlemen, up to now we have buried you without coffins[1] or crosses. Now you will be buried with coffins and crosses as decreed by the new "Frontführer"'.

The person who gave out the mocking 'spiel' was an officer prisoner-of-war turned traitor, by the name of Shibayev. There were a few like him on Alderney who, glad to save their own skins, were ready to become toadies of the Germans.

I remember, for instance, the Priakhims, father and son from Helgoland camp. The son became a guard and bullied his own father.

Former prisoners of Norderney, Ivan Dolgov and Kirill Nevrov, told of another traitor – the interpreter Boris 'Squab' (Short arse). This was his nickname, they couldn't remember his surname. This swine liked to beat his victims about the face, but because of his low stature, could only enjoy his favorite pastime by standing on a stool.

Not all those working for the Germans distinguished themselves by their bestial cruelty. I must mention the interpreter Fyedya who saved more than one life in Alderney, my own included. One evening as I was passing the commandant's house I noticed that something was thrown out of the window. Pushing my way on all fours under the barbed wire I saw some scraps of bread and a half-eaten bunch of grapes. I swallowed the bread in a flash, but I just gaped at the grapes. Felix Kosoy, the deputy commandant of the camp, caught me immediately, and cried out '*Dolmetscher!*' ('Interpreter!'). Fyedya came running. I knew perfectly well that for such an action I would be carried out half dead, and my stomach contracted within me.

'What were you doing under the commandant's windows?' I opened my hand holding the bunch of grapes. 'So, you wanted to eat them ?' Here Fyedya came to my help. According to his translation I didn't understand or know what grapes were, and had picked up the bunch simply out of curiosity. In this the interpreter was partly correct, I had indeed never before eaten grapes. To my eternal astonishment and joy, they turned me towards the gate and gave me a very firm kick – which by their standards was the greatest act of mercy.

---

[1] After the liberation of Alderney, British soldiers found a 're-usable' double height coffin, the bottom of which opened to allow the bodies to drop out and the coffin to be re-used, in the grass round the Russian graves on Longis Common.

After Alderney much more happened to me which I could talk about: my time in the French Resistance, the joy of Victory, post-war devastation and the long years of being treated as inadequate by friends and relations. In those days in the fifties, the very word 'repatriated' was almost synonymous with 'enemy of the people'. Even to this day attitudes towards people such as myself are mixed. Indeed this is why former prisoners in German camps do not usually like to talk of that terrible time.

However, there are various reasons for everything: the inhuman conditions of captivity in themselves brought out not only the best in people, but also at times the worst.

Despite all this I have decided to write about what I remember myself and what my comrades have told me. I wish that people who have never seen war (Thank God) should know more about it. Maybe then young people will treat those of the war generation with greater interest and respect, maybe then the young people of Orel will at last stop walking their dogs in the modest little memorial garden, situated in the centre of our town, in the very place where, during the war there was a prisoner-of-war camp where 5,000 men were tortured . . . perhaps we may see the like another time – and one's heart stops, not only from pain, but weakness.

G. Kondakov.

In personal communications with the author, Georgi Kondakov has given some details of himself.

He was born on 7 December 1925 in the village of Merzalovka, and went to the town of Orel (birthplace of Russian author Turgenev) in 1940 to the *Reushniki* or Craftsmen School. After the Germans entered Orel on 4 October 1940 they started to deport young people for labour in Germany.

Kondakov was taken, and eventually arrived in Alderney in August 1942 aged 16, with a total of about 1,000 prisoners from the Orel region. After they were shipped off to France in 1943, when some of the slaves were evacuated from Alderney, he escaped from a German camp and joined the Resistance. He took part in the rebellion in Paris, and continued to work there for the Allies after it was freed, as adjutant to the commander of the Russian ex-prisoners assembly point. In May 1945 he returned to Russia to find everything destroyed. In 1947, with many other ex-prisoners of the Nazis, he was arrested and spent $4\frac{1}{2}$ years in a Stalinist camp, north of the Arctic Circle. He married in 1955, has two children and a grandchild. He retired in 1985 and bought a piece of land where he grows vegetables and keeps bees. He and his wife and family live in a State-owned, three-roomed flat.

In January 1990, after months of negotiations, and applications for travel permits, Georgi was able to return to Alderney as a guest of the States, and revisit the scenes of his former captivity. A full account of his experiences in Alderney during the war, and his feelings on return, is given in *The Island of Dread in the Channel*, published in 1991.

CHAPTER ELEVEN

The Slave Workers

John Dalmau was an officer of the Spanish Republican Army who, after being wounded in January 1939 in a skirmish near the French frontier, got over the border and later joined the French Army. He was captured by the Germans in Luxembourg in the spring of 1940, and sent in December to join the labour gangs working on Hitler's Atlantic Wall. Some months later he was sent to Jersey, part of a contingent of about 2,000 Spanish OT workers. In early 1943 he was transferred to Alderney via France and Guernsey, and employed first on converting two houses in Victoria Street into a hospital[1] and then on maintenance work at the harbour, including repairs to damaged ships.

A German convoy in Braye Bay, January 1943

[1]This presumably refers to repairs to the existing Mignot Memorial Hospital there.

He was in a camp with people from many nationalities, and a number of Jews who apparently received worse treatment than the others. He also confirms that the Vichy French were allowed home on leave every three or four months and were well paid.

Later, while working on Fort Albert, Dalmau claims that many slaves too weak to work were thrown over the cliff and that one day fifty were shot and thrown over. While diving to carry out repairs to the harbour boom, he says he saw masses of skeletons and bloated corpses among the seaweed on the sea bed, with lobsters and crabs feeding on them. He also makes record of both mass and individual shootings of political prisoners and Jews, especially following reports of Allied raids on German towns.

By fishing for conger and making an octopus trap, Dalmau and his friends managed to augment their rations considerably, and there were apparently plenty of octopus around at that period, even in the Old Harbour. On 2 May 1944 he states that he killed one measuring just over 15 ft across.

Dalmau records many air-raid warnings during his time in Alderney, and saw and heard gunfire on D-Day, shortly after which the Germans evacuated most of the slaves. The first to go were the political prisoners and Jews on two boats to St Malo via Guernsey. The boats then returned to Alderney and evacuated most of the remaining Spaniards, French, Dutch, Belgians and Russians. They were taken to St Peter Port in Guernsey, losing contact *en route* with a boat containing most of the French women from Alderney.

In Guernsey they continued to work on harbour maintenance until the surrender. Two days after his arrival, Dalmau records that HMS *Rodney* shelled Alderney and the explosions were felt in Guernsey. The action was taken to silence the battery on The Giffoine[2] which had been shelling the area around Cherbourg, by then in Allied hands. It is stated in his book, that three of the four guns were rendered inoperable in an action lasting a couple of hours, during which seventy-five 1 ton shells were fired into Alderney, from 20 miles away on the other side of the Cotentin peninsula.

Dalmau also claims that, of about 4,000 Spaniards in the Channel Islands, only fifty-nine survived. He later married a Guernsey girl, and wrote his little sixteen page pamphlet, *Slave Worker in the Channel Islands*, in, presumably, the 1950s although the work itself bears no date. The foreword was written by the Lt.-Governor of Guernsey, Sir Thomas Elmhirst, who was in office in 1954.

The story is taken up by Norbert Beernaert, one of the Belgian prisoners, who was brought to the island in mid-December 1940, aged 16, in the early days of the German occupation.

---

[2] This occurred on 12 August 1944, and was actually the Rond But, Batterie Blücher.

Slave workers building a gun emplacement by the light railway at Fort Albert, 1942

As recorded in Steckoll's book, at this time Beernaert was not restricted in movement about the island, and for a few weeks had nothing to do until the *Organisation Todt* arrived. He helped unload the ships which brought the huts used to build Norderney camp, and the Belgian workers who erected them. He worked for a short time for a German officer, billeted at the old barracks behind what is now the Essex Manor Restaurant, by Longis Bay, and was then moved to Norderney. At that time, or shortly after, Norderney was under the command of elderly SS *Obersturmführer* Adler.

After about six months Beernaert was sent to Guernsey for a few weeks, to a cookery school, and then returned to Alderney. He states that, at this time, the various parties (or 'firms') of volunteer *Todt* workers were generally only in the Norderney camp for short periods of time, returning to Europe when the job they were contracted to do was completed. In this way the Belgians were replaced in turn by Spaniards, then Africans and Seneghalese, Czechs, Dutch and lastly Swedes. These were finally succeeded by Russians and Ukrainians, at which time their movements became restricted, and they were not allowed to leave the area round the camp. Early in 1942 he was moved to a camp behind the abattoir in Le Val (possibly *Lager Citadella*), where he was employed as cook to a party of German civilians, who were well fed. They were some sort of specialists, and he found out later they had been making parts for V1 rockets (flying or 'buzz'-bombs).

Another prisoner in Norderney was Francisco Font, also a former soldier of the Spanish Republican Army, handed over to the Germans by the Vichy French, who settled in Jersey after the war. In 1951 he told Solomon Steckoll that he was brought to Alderney in October 1943. He was employed at the harbour and around the island as a bricklayer or mason, and had to march to work and back every day. His stories about the rations they got, and the conditions they lived under, agree closely with those already given, and he too told of the brutality of some of the guards, the 'kapos', and the disposal of many bodies in the sea, especially from Sylt camp. With most of the other prisoners he was taken to Guernsey a few days after D-Day, and then to Jersey. By the time he was due to be taken on to St Malo, it was in Allied hands and he was kept in Jersey until the surrender.

Mr Gordon Prigent, a Jerseyman sent to Alderney as a punishment late in 1943, spent some time in Sylt and was later imprisoned at Norderney, with a party of five other Channel Islanders. They were employed as agricultural workers on the fields on The Blayes and in the Valley Gardens, staying overnight in The 1720 House, or on unloading ships at the harbour, and transporting the food to St Anne. After D-Day he says that all food was stored under guard at Fort Albert. They were not allowed to talk to other prisoners and knew little about what went on elsewhere in the island. He did, however, see two Americans who were imprisoned at Sylt and the two Chinese reported from other sources at Norderney. He also mentioned Irish volunteer workers, billeted at Château à L'Etoc. On his visit to Alderney in April 1978 Prigent gave further details of a bombing raid in St Anne on D-Day when a bomb was dropped in the Valley Gardens and cannon shells damaged The 1720 House. He says that they saw gliders passing over on their way to Normandy and saw them released. He also reports a party of Italian sailors quartered at the Drewitt's house in Connaught Square, and tells that, after D-Day, whenever there was a night alarm at Norderney all prisoners had to collect within two minutes in the tunnel to Arch Bay. If Allied troops landed nearby, all the prisoners were to be shot. Perhaps this is what gave rise to the stories about the tunnel. Mr Prigent was taken with other slaves to Guernsey and on to Jersey *en route* for France at the end of June 1944, after Cherbourg had been captured by the Americans. As the RAF had sunk so many ships between Jersey and France he remained in Jersey.

A French prisoner, Jean Delourmée, a carpenter from Dinan, was brought to Alderney with about twenty-five other Frenchmen, on the MV *Robert Müller* in March 1943 at the age of 20. He was originally housed in Norderney. He states that there were then ninety-two Frenchmen in the camp, and that in August 1943 about 200 French Jews were brought in. Well dressed, on their arrival they were adorned with a white paint stripe, painted down each side of their clothes from shoulder to ankle. His description of their conditions and rations agrees very closely with the others, but he adds that the French were better treated than the Russians, or the German political prisoners. He was employed in the camp workshop by the OT firm 'Wolfgang Goebbels', making shuttering and window frames for the concrete bunkers. The German iron jetty was being built during his time here.

Like many of the other prisoners Delourmée fell ill with boils, was looked after by a Russian doctor, and after three weeks in 'hospital', was shipped to Cherbourg by night to be sent to Germany. He escaped *en route* and returned to a place about 15 miles from his home, where he hid for the remainder of the war.

Also in 1943, after negotiation with the Jersey authorities, the Germans brought over a party of fifty workers to repair houses on Alderney. They were supposed to be paid volunteers, but in the event only about twenty volunteers were recruited, and a further thirty conscripted to make up the numbers required. Another Frenchman, Fisch Marcel, brought to Alderney in September 1943 to work in the quarries, was sent to Germany on 5 May 1944, when he says work on the fortifications ceased or was completed.

There seems to be general agreement that the camps were evacuated and most of the SS guards removed around D-Day, although there is a report in *The Alderney Story*, that Helgoland was evacuated and burnt in October 1943. Aerial photographs taken by 541 Squadron RAF on 12 June 1944, however, clearly show all of the huts at Helgoland standing and undamaged. Further pictures from the same source, taken on 29 May 1945, show about half of the huts destroyed and overgrown, which would seem to confirm their disbandment after D-Day.

The usual route taken by the prison ships was via Guernsey to St Malo, sometimes by way of Jersey, and there are various reports of ships containing prisoners, and the camp women, being sunk by the British on the way. One, the SS *Minotaure* which was carrying 500, mostly Jewish, prisoners from Alderney, was sunk with three of her small German escorts between St Helier and St Malo, and about 250 of the prisoners perished, an episode documented by a survivor. Another, *Gerfried*, took 280 Russian prisoners from Alderney to St Malo via Guernsey and Jersey. The journey took from 24 June to 1 July. Other ships involved in this transfer included *Schwalbe*, *Lena*, *Spinel*, and *Franka*.

Many of those prisoners who did reach mainland France, particularly those from Sylt, were then carried across France to Germany by train, and many died in the over-crowded carriages. Their journey back across Europe and later around Germany has already been described. The few survivors were rescued by American forces at Remingsdorf-Steyr on 5 May 1945, almost a year after they left Alderney.

CHAPTER TWELVE

The Captors

As we have seen already, from the group of about eighty soldiers and airmen who first occupied the island, numbers had risen by July 1941 to about 450, and by November, following Hitler's orders to increase the defences, to 2,426 men.

Of this number many were Naval personnel, responsible for the manning of the larger gun batteries which were being constructed on The Giffoine (Anne Batterie) and Fort Albert (Elsass), and air force personnel who manned the anti-aircraft guns. At about this time (November 1941) the airport was made useless by a number of trenches being dug across it. Clearly shown on aerial photographs taken by 541 Squadron RAF, the pattern they make bears a marked similarity to the lines of the three runways present today, although at the beginning of the war there was only a single landing strip.

Then, as now, the runway covered much of the best agricultural land of the island, and parts were used to grow the wheat and oats needed by the garrison. The earlier agreement to grow food to transport to Guernsey to help feed the civilian population there was apparently ignored after the departure of the Guernsey agricultural party.

In December 1983 the Alderney Museum received two albums of photographs, well mounted and documented, from a former soldier of the Alderney garrison, Helmut Asbeck, who had been a member of the Army Coastal Artillery Unit's Batterie Blücher. Like Herr Herzog, his recollections and photographs have provided valuable information and resources, and are gratefully acknowledged.

Asbeck's unit, formerly at Le Havre, arrived in Alderney aboard the freighter *Lena* on 22 July 1941 about sunset, and was marched to Fort Tourgis where they were to be billeted. Shortly afterwards Asbeck had to man a temporary observation post on the eastern edge of St Anne. They set up their stereoscope in a field, and camouflaged it with branches. The party of four men lodged in a house in Longis Road. This only lasted a little while, however, until they established a permanent post at a house on the south cliffs, which, from his description and photographs, is the coastguard look-out. Formerly on top of Essex Hill, but long since been demolished, only part of the metal railings remain today.

During their time here the unit used off-duty periods to catch lobsters in Longis Bay and around Raz Island. Along the cliff path Asbeck came across the

The old coastguard station on Essex Hill, July 1941

A shell hitting 'Hanging Rock' during target practice, taken from the window of Fort Essex

'Hanging Rock', and, hearing that the Naval Coastal Artillery were proposing to blast away the upper part to improve their field of fire, he managed to secure the dramatic shot, from a window of Fort Essex, of a shell hitting the rock.

Their rations were still cooked at Fort Tourgis, and carried to St Anne from whence they fetched them. Their post was to be connected to the telephone cable being laid all round the island to link the posts to the command centre and they had to dig the trench for it themselves. Later, with the erection of a flak battery (anti-aircraft) nearby they were able to get their food with the gunners.

From time to time Asbeck's group had to go to the harbour to help unload stores. By the description he gives, the Germans were still using the commercial quay at this stage. With its two levels, Asbeck thought it very well designed. From other sources it has been stated that the larger ships could only berth here during about two hours at each high tide, thus limiting its use, and the sectional jetty did not arrive until 22 May 1942.

On one of his trips to the harbour, Asbeck met an 'Alderney Farmer', to whom he refers as Mr John, 'the only inhabitant of Alderney who had stayed in the island'. It is not clear whether this name was a Christian or a surname, but none of the local people already recorded as staying bore either name.

Freighters and harbour patrol boats at the jetty, 1942

His battery was given two spells of home leave during his time here. In September 1941 they were taken direct to Cherbourg, and returned the same way. At the second leave, in February 1942, he went to Cherbourg by night for two weeks leave, returning overland from Cherbourg to Granville, and then by boat to Jersey–Guernsey–Alderney, because, 'The direct passage from Alderney to Cherbourg was no longer safe for us'.

This statement is confirmed from other sources, as has already been noted. The British had sunk the German ships *Hermann* and *Schleswig Holstein*, both motor vessels, *en route* between Alderney and Cherbourg in a surface battle on 3 February 1942.

At Easter 1942 Asbeck and some companions were to go to Guernsey in the Dutch coaster *RO8*, whose proper designation was SS *Irene*. Their departure was delayed and they cooked their food on a field kitchen on the deck. During this short time, while waiting for the ship to sail, he visited Crabby and Clonque Bays.

The photo through the stereo was apparently taken by a comrade and copied by Asbeck, which no doubt accounts for its poorer quality. The various views taken about the town and island, by Asbeck and other, unknown, photographers, all date from this period.

An 88 mm anti-aircraft gun on Essex Hill, viewed through a stereo range-finder

A German band outside the Island HQ, June 1941

Asbeck makes no complaint about the rations they were getting in this comparatively early part of the occupation, nor about the posting, which, in retrospect some forty years later, he obviously did not regard as a punishment, even though he only received two spells of two weeks home leave. He makes no mention at all of camps or prisoners, while Nebel, arriving in March 1942 before Asbeck left, tells quite a different story, as we have seen.

Easter 1942 also saw the first formal large parade of German troops in the island. The column marched along Church Street, through Connaught Square and the salute was taken in Marais Square. (Some of the pictures taken of this event have been reproduced previously.) After the parade, the band gave a concert outside 515 Civil Affairs Unit HQ at Lloyds Bank, and also outside the *Inselkommandant's* HQ in Connaught Square.

Posted to Alderney on 10 July 1942 was an old soldier, born near Hanover in January 1889, *Hauptruppführer* Gustav Dahmer, who had served on the Russian front in the First World War, and had helped in the building of the Siegfried Line (West Wall) in 1938. After serving in various building and stores battalions, Dahmer had arrived in Guernsey, where he worked in the pay office of the *Todt*

Organisation for the firm Ackermann. Being unwise enough to make disparaging remarks about the German minister of food, Durer, which were overheard by an informer, he was brought up before a court martial of the 319 Infantry Division. He was acquitted by this *Wehrmacht* court. In his diary Dahmer notes, 'Had I come before an SS Court it might have cost me my head' – a comment he repeats in various documents and letters he wrote both while in Alderney and after the war. These he gave to the museum, together with his medals, and those of his sons, one *Gefreite* (Lt.-Cpl.) Helmuth Dahmer who was killed on the Russian front by partisans while Dahmer was in Guernsey, and the other *Gefreite* Gunther Dahmer who died in a Russian prison camp.

Appointed as a construction group commander, Dahmer came to Alderney via Cherbourg, having to wait nineteen days there for a ship:

The ship service to Alderney was really lamentable. One could never be sure when one could land, sometimes due to U-boat danger, sometimes rough seas or the nights too light, and so on. Once they forgot to enter me

Helmut Lücke, a soldier in the *Voorpostenboote* (the Harbour Guardships), in Alderney, 1944

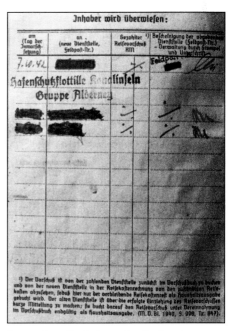

A page from Lücke's pay-book, showing posting to Alderney, 10 July 1942

on the ship's list. . . . It certainly was a God-forsaken island. Weeks without post. To write to my two boys in Russia took a month to receive an answer. We could send our relations nothing as there was nothing to send. The construction firms at least had canteens which obtained supplies from the mainland, albeit at unheard of prices. I noted in my diary of 21.8.42 that I paid 90 Reichmarks for a pound of coffee and 112.7 for a pound of tea. One was glad when one could send it home or to the East Front . . . Once 200 men going home on leave were torpedoed by an English ship, and another time a ship was wrecked on the cliffs of Guernsey. Of the SS we saw little. They were there to guard the inmates of the concentration camps. There were too, Russian prisoners who were in misery. They looked for food remains from our barracks. One hears that four to six men died daily. Only after complaints from the Russian doctor who was there, was it supposed to improve . . .

16.4.43. There is no drink on the island. Great despondency as most cannot live without drink.

At several places in his narrative there are comments about the bad treatment of prisoners by the SS, and beatings by their own 'boss' leaders or 'kapos'. He also mentions frequent problems with supplies which got sent to the wrong place, or diverted to unauthorized channels. Large maps of England, scale 1:100,000, prepared for the invasion, were taken as souvenirs. The pieces of equipment sent to Alderney for the newly-built slaughter-house were not the right machines: 'perhaps the others were bought on the black market in France'.

Fairly early on during Dahmer's time in Alderney, the confirmation of his acquittal arrived from the HQ of the *Todt Organisation* in Normandy, and is preserved with the other papers, as is his leave pass for two weeks from 14 June 1943.

Dahmer had spent his birthday on 31 January 1943 in Cherbourg on duty. Men returning from Christmas leave had been delayed there for weeks. They all finally sailed on the 800 ton ship *Tinda* on 3 February. Also on board the ship were a party of Czech construction technicians, and a variety troop '(Strength through Pleasure). Only a mediocre performance', but they seem to have had a very convivial evening in the end. The variety troop were stuck on Alderney for two weeks before a boat came to take them off. The performance must have been similar to that in the photographs taken at Fort Albert in the summer of 1941.

An interesting document, dating from 30 November 1943 and concerning the rations to which the men were entitled at that time, came to light in 1980, found in a drawer in an old piece of furniture. Issued from Divisional HQ and

Gustav Dahmer's leave pass

The German concert party at Fort Albert, summer 1941

addressed to the Quartermaster's Branch of the 319th Infantry Division, the document was signed by Engelbert, the Divisional supply officer, and approved by the paymaster, Lt. Schnee. The subject of the document was *Weihnachttszuwendungen* – Christmas allocations.

Additional rations were to be issued at Christmas 1943 to all officers and men, military officials and members of the foreign volunteer units. POWs, French and British nationals employed by the units were specifically excluded from these benefits. The rations comprised:

> 500 gm Christmas cake and pastries
> 125 gm biscuits (1 packet)
> 120 gm sweets
> 250 gm apples
> ¼ litre brandy

A further 1 Reichsmark per head was allowed for Christmas decorations, and there was to be one Christmas candle for every three men. It was doubted whether there could be a delivery of Christmas trees.

During this same period in Alderney, according to another document found at the same time, there appear to have been two ration scales in use – scale 3 and scale 1. This second document sets out the daily rations for each individual meal, and includes a synopsis of the totals for the week.

In summary, scale 3 rations per man per week consisted of:

Bread, 4,900 gm; meat, 400 gm; sausage, 300 gm; vegetables, including onions, 2,435 gm; peas, 150 gm; potatoes, 4,200 gm; coffee substitute, 63 gm; tea substitute, 4 gm; butter, 200 gm; jam 400 gm; frying fat, 10 gm; cheese, 100 gm; pastries, 225 gm; pudding powder, 20 gm; gravy powder, 70 gm; sugar, 230 gm; salt, 140 gm; semolina, 50 gm; sweets, 30 gm; cinnamon, 0.25 gm; paprika, 0.15 gm; tomato puree 10 gm; pepper, 0.05 gm; vinegar, 0.2l gm; soup seasoning 3 gm; caraway seeds, 0.5 gm; bay leaves, 0.05 gm; soda water, ½ bottle; 12 cigarettes and 2 small cigars.

Scale 1 rations carried, in addition, an extra 290 gm meat and 60 gm sausage, 1 portion of fish, 50 gm butter, 70 gm sugar, 20 gm gravy powder, an extra 12 cigarettes, 2 cigars and 17 gm of tobacco. The cinnamon and semolina, however, were not allowed! It is not clear who was intended to benefit from the larger rations, but presumably the officers.

Troops receiving these rations (if they actually got them) would have been well fed, and the earlier complaints of Gerhard Nebel would certainly not have been justified in late 1943. After D-Day, of course, no further supplies reached the island and things would have taken on a very different complexion.

A weekly order sheet for the 584 Grenadier (Infantry) Regiment, consisting of 1 officer and 120 other ranks, stationed at Türkenburg (Fort Tourgis) has survived, dated 7–13 May 1944.

Headed *Wochendienstplan für die Zeit vom 7–13.5.44* (Daily Workplan for the week 7–13 May 1944), it shows that the unit was engaged on *Stellungsbau* (building fortifications) daily including Sunday from 7 a.m. to noon. There was a break until 1.30 p.m., and a daily cleaning of weapons and ammunition from 7–8.30 p.m. except on Saturday and Sunday. Four days in the week there was weapons training at their action stations from 1.30–2.30 p.m. followed by fortification building to 6 p.m. On Sunday, the period from midday was used to repair clothing and equipment, and there was a kit inspection from 2.30–3 p.m., the remainder of the day being free. On Saturdays from 1.30–3 p.m. there was company instructions and a current affairs talk at Fort Tourgis given by Lt. Kramer, the company commander. Weapons were cleaned from 3–4 p.m after which two hours were devoted to cleaning the living quarters in the fort and bathing. Supper was taken daily from 6–7 p.m.

This document shows clearly that construction of fortifications was continuing at least to a couple of weeks before D-Day.

Dahmer also refers to the Saturday afternoon talk by Kramer and notes how the men hated to go to it.

After the war many claims were made by both officers and men of the *Wehrmacht*, the regular army, that they did not know what was going on in the camps, or that it was nothing to do with them. At the time of the surrender, the Commanding Officer, Lt.-Col. Schwalm, claimed that Maj. Hoffmann had taken all the OT records with him when he left the island.

The odd comment from various ex-prisoners supports the idea that some of the ordinary troops exhibited a degree of kindness and sympathy towards the slaves. With their freedom to move about the island in no way restricted, it seems impossible, however, that all of the garrison should not have been aware of the conditions existing in the island. They could scarcely have failed to notice the poor physical condition of the 'workers', which Dahmer had certainly noted.

In an order from HQ 43rd Army Corps dated 2.6.41, which covered all of the islands, it is noted that, at that time, Alderney was under the command of 216 Division, as well as the Coastal Artillery Commander in Cherbourg.

The island commander was the Cdr. Naval Coast Battery. Of troops there was one platoon – IR348 of 216 Div; one reinforced platoon – IR257; and one 17 cm coastal battery.

On 26.6.41 the commander reported:

Present status: one coastal battery completed.
Most of shelters for fire direction, crew, and ammunition complete.

By mid-July 1941 a further report stated:

Construction group 1/14 arrived. Reinforcements transferred: Army Coastal Battery 461 with 4 x 15 cm K 18 guns installed.

By this time there were about 2,500 troops stationed on Alderney, although this was soon increased as already noted. The roll of troops in the island in September 1944 consisted of 3,201 men, made up as follows:

890 Infantry; 590 Navy, employed on the coastal batteries and harbour duties; 1,051 Air Force, manning anti-aircraft defences, which obviously had a high priority (there were no flying personnel); 70 Artillery (Battery Blücher); 200 Service Corps; 400 others probably ancillaries, medics, etc.

By this date most of the SS would have gone, with the removal of the majority of the prisoners and slaves in June and July 1944.

German papers from the Bailiff's office in Guernsey, dated 1 September 1944, show that the strength of troops was calculated on the basis of one battalion per 13 km of coastline for each of the three main islands. Alderney, with 17 km of coast, had a battalion plus one company. The papers also record that, in the loss of the *Hermann* and *Schleswig Holstein* in February 1942, 150 men going on leave died, that there were eight naval engagements up to that time, five of them between Alderney and Cherbourg, and that two of the ships stranded in Alderney were a total loss.

At the time of the surrender the following May, about 3,000 men were left on the island. The majority of these (some 2,332, including about 175 or so stretcher cases from the hospitals and sick quarters) were taken to England in five landing craft in the following few days, as POWs.

The remaining troops and the now ex-slaves were kept employed in cleaning up the island, removing mines and obstructions, and carrying on the necessary agricultural work.

The captors were now the captured, and the worst of Alderney's ordeal was over.

CHAPTER THIRTEEN

The Defences

Soon after they occupied the island, it became obvious to the German forces that the harbour facilities were inadequate for the amount of shipping needed to transport all the materials they wanted, and that the stone jetty was only accessible to larger ships for about one or two hours each side of high water.

The failure of Hitler's invasion to take place after Dunkirk, had resulted, by the spring of 1941, in the standing down of the troops along the Channel coast and the dispersal of the thousands of barges prepared for transporting them. Hitler, nevertheless, had not entirely abandoned the idea of invading England at some future date, and various preparations were still being made. Now, however, all of Europe was subjugated by the Germans, and the only threats to their domination came from the Eastern Front and the Russians, and from across the Channel in England. America, at this time, was still neutral.

By the end of June 1941 the Army Coastal Artillery Battery No. 461 was complete and operational and all the ancillary trenches, ammunition stores, and shelters built. It consisted of 4 x 15 cm K 18 guns sited at Le Rond But, and was generally referred to as Batterie Blücher.

By the end of July 1941, the anti-aircraft batteries were combat ready, and the 1st Battalion reserve AA Battalion 496, with 88 mm guns, and the 2nd platoon of the 3rd Battalion 731, with 20 mm light AA guns, were in place. By now the German garrison numbered approximately 2,500 men.

A request was sent for two 6 ton motor tractors for Howitzer Batteries to be supplied to Alderney.

On 9.9.41 a report to Army High Command 15 stated that the north coast of Alderney was the most likely target for attack from the sea, and that Alderney was also a favourable spot for an airborne landing. Another request was submitted for 1 battery of 4 x 38 cm guns, 2 batteries of 4 x 15 cm SK c/28 guns, a reinforced company of infantry, 1 platoon tanks, 1 platoon engineers.

As we have already seen, on 18.10.41 the Führer directed that all defences were to be increased. The old forts were to be used, and the captured Russian 17 cm guns installed at Fort Albert and Le Rond But were to be replaced with 15 cm SK c/28 guns. He further directed that, to achieve this, his engineers may get skilled workers from Russian POW camps, use skilled 'Red' Spaniards

A sketch drawn in 1945 of the
searchlight battery hidden in the cliff
above Cachalière

especially, and they were to create all-round fields of fire for the batteries.
Flanking batteries were to be placed at all bays and beaches.

The result of this order is still to be seen everywhere on Alderney, even by the
casual observer.

America only entered the war after the Japanese attack on Pearl Harbour on
7 December 1941. Hitler, who was in no way committed to support Japan,
made the mistake of immediately declaring war on the United States, an action
which eventually cost him dear.

By the time the relieving forces came in 1945 and found the jetty in position,
it had of course already been noted in aerial surveys and plotted on their maps.
Speculation was rife as to its originally intended purpose, however. It was
eventually decided that it had been designed to fill in the gaps in Brighton Pier
(made as a defensive precaution by the English), when the Germans invaded
England. It was not until well after it had finally been demolished, in 1978, that
an extensive piece of research by Dr Peter Schenk into the proposed invasion of

England (Operation Sealion) for his book, *Landung in England*, published in Berlin in 1987, revealed its true origins.

In preparation for the future invasion of England, two types of sectional jetty which could be towed into position and rapidly sited and assembled for use, had been designed. The different units were designed by the Dortmunder Union Company, and by Krupp's, whose design proved to be the simpler and more rapid to erect.

They were to provide deep water landing facilities for men and equipment. The prototypes had been assembled in the North Sea and withstood the winter of 1941/2. By this time, however, the changed circumstances had prompted the decision to fortify the coast, from Norway to Spain, against any British counter-attack in the future.

Late in 1941 it was decided to use these units, no more of which were to be made, and to bring the prototypes of the landing piers to Alderney to extend the jetty into deeper water. The Alderney jetty was made from portions of these two different types of unit. Once in position the telescopic legs were set down on the sea bed. They were then permanently fixed by posts rammed into the bed, and subsequently raised hydraulically, releasing the ships which had delivered them, and allowing the units to be levelled and aligned. The different units were then

A German jetty, November 1945

linked by bridging sections. They were taken down from the North Sea in March and April 1942, and the Dortmunder Union sections arrived in Alderney on 26 May followed, about ten days later, by the Krupp sections. By September the construction was completed using Belgian technicians and welders. It is said that local divers and engineers from Guernsey were also employed in this work. Further sections of these units were found in France in the late 1960s.

The jetty now in place, with three large French cranes mounted on it in April 1943, and a mobile Russian one to support them, the German forces were able to bring in supplies, reinforcements, and workers at any time. Several ships could berth at once, and heavy equipment could be unloaded easily.

By May 1943 a garrison of 3,800 was needed to operate and service all the weapons and the equipment, and to control the men building and installing the jetty and the guns.

The German papers from the Bailiff's archives (mentioned previously) list the defences of Alderney at 1 September 1944, in addition to the heavy batteries listed below, as three heavy *Flieger Abwehr Kanone* (AA guns) [88 mm] per sq km, six times the density in Guernsey, and nine times that of Jersey. There was, in addition, an allocation of three light AA guns to every heavy one.

At the time of the surrender the summary of the completed defences of Alderney, as found on the ground by the relieving forces, was as follows:

Artillery Batteries:

Battery	Position	Operator	Guns	Range
Annes	on The Giffoine	Navy	4 x 15 cm C/28	22,000 m
Blücher	at Le Rond But	Army	4 x 15 cm K 18	24,800 m
Elsass	on Fort Albert	Navy	3 x 17 cm SK L/40	22,000 m
Falke	mobile battery		4 x 10 cm FH 14/19	9,600 m
Marcks	fixed battery		4 x 10.5 cm K 331	8,200 m

Plus, in individual casemates spaced out, 8 x 10.5 cm K 331 guns, range 8,200 m

The first three batteries (Annes, Blücher and Elsass) were controlled from the fire control tower at Mannez.

Anti-Aircraft Batteries:

3 batteries of 6 x 88 mm heavy AA guns
3 batteries of 3 x 37 mm light AA guns
11 batteries of 3 x 20 mm light AA guns

There were, in addition, a number of 75 mm, 50 mm and 47 mm anti-tank guns sited in the bays and in the sea wall at Longis, several mounted searchlights on tracks, radar units, and numerous machine gun nests and strong points in most of the old forts and scattered over the island. The maps show the general distribution of these weapons.

It is interesting to note, also at the time of the surrender, that the Naval fire control tower (*Marinepeilstand*), standing above Mannez Quarry with three levels, each controlling one battery, was only one of six such projected for Alderney, and that barely two-fifths of the total defences in the final plan had actually been built. In part this was due to the withdrawal, around D-Day, of much of the slave-labour force, and the difficulty of bringing in supplies, especially of cement and steel, which had considerably slowed things. Also of course, only half of the eight year time schedule for the completion of the impregnable defences of Europe had passed. Even so, there was almost as much hardware installed on this tiny island as on each of the two larger islands.

Marinepeilstand ('The Odeon'), Mannez, 1945

CHAPTER FOURTEEN

The Enemy under Attack

During the occupation, many air sorties were made over Alderney. A considerable number were carried out in order to obtain photographic evidence of the defences of the island to assist the possible future invasion, and the final compendium of these was collected into a map which was overlaid on the old 1911 survey to produce a secret map, which was prepared for D-Day.

The shooting down of the two Spitfires over Longis and Braye in November 1941, and the commando raids on The Casquets and Burhou, have been previously mentioned, as has the sinking, in surface action off Alderney on

The burial of casualties from the sinking of motor vessels *Hermann* and *Schleswig Holstein* by motor torpedo-boats on 3 February 1942. The funeral took place at the German Cemetery at Valongis

3 February 1942, of two German motorcoasters, *Schleswig Holstein* and *Hermann*, both of 174 tons, *en route* between Cherbourg and Alderney. This action was the result of frequent sorties by the Royal Navy into the area, often with fast motor torpedo boats (MTBs).

The Germans had taken to running their freighters from Cherbourg to Alderney at night in convoys of four or five, and, as they were approaching the island, the lighthouse and the leading lights in Braye Bay were turned on to guide them in. This was used by the Royal Navy as a signal and they knew that ships were approaching, enabling them to slip in and catch the enemy unawares.

The 109 ton tug *Thor* had previously been sunk between Alderney and Cap de la Hague, on 10 December 1940, and in another action just north of Alderney on 9 September 1942, the 300 ton former Dutch MV *Henca* was part of a small convoy of two coasters and two escorts which were bombed by the RAF. After being hit, *Henca* capsized and sank. A month later, on 6 October, the barge *Marcelle* was in a collision and sank.

There were a few bombing raids made, and there was a report of a bomb falling behind the *Soldatenheim* in November 1942 when every German officer was inside at a conference. There were no reports of any casualties.

A number of the recorded comments of members of the German garrison are concerned with the frequency of night alerts. It is at least possible that most of these occurred because of aircraft passing over Alderney on their way to bomb targets on the mainland of Europe, although aerial photographs of the area round the airfield taken about D-Day clearly show clusters of bomb craters, most likely the result of a single raid. As the airfield was not apparently used by the occupying forces after their early landings, and the trenches dug across the area rendered it virtually useless, this would seem to have been rather pointless from a practical point of view.

VP 703 (*Vorpostenboot* or Outpost Boat) and the 301 ton *Henny Fricke* whose keels and boilers, as already noted, are still to be seen at low tide on the rocks in the middle of the bay, sank in Braye Harbour on 14 January 1943. On the same day the 49 ton *Notre Dame de la Délivérance* struck a rock and sank north of Alderney.

The final record of enemy shipping sunk around our shores during this period was in the surface battle on 16 April 1944, when the 670 ton minesweeper *M 83* was sunk.

Steckoll reports that a Lancaster bomber ditched in the sea off Alderney on 27 July 1944, and that the crew were subsequently 'murdered' by Korvette Kapitan Massmann, the harbour commandant. It is certainly documented in German sources that, after the plane ditched, Massmann refused to allow a boat to be launched to pick up the survivors, who presumably drowned.

The principal action against the island was that which took place on 12 August 1944. At this time the long range guns of the army coastal battery Blücher, situated on Le Rond But just south of St Anne and with a range of 24,800 metres, were shelling the landing beaches some miles west of Cherbourg, and had to be silenced. HMS *Rodney* was ordered to carry out this action, and made an approach to Alderney on about 8/9 August. Good visibility at the time was thought to make the job of the RAF Spitfires, acting as spotter planes, too hazardous in view of the intensive concentration of anti-aircraft batteries on Alderney, and they were turned back. Three days later the bombardment was carried out from the other side of the Cherbourg Peninsula, about 20 miles away, out of sight of the island. A report from John Moroso who was on board, published in the *Daily Telegraph* on 16 August, records the action:

> During a period of two and a half hours, seventy-five 1 ton shells were pumped into Alderney, starting at 2.11 p.m. The Germans were apparently caught by surprise, and no return fire was experienced.

The report continues:

> . . . our first shot landed 300 yards from the target, we corrected the range, and on the fifth, sixth, seventh and eighth shots made direct hits on the Nazi guns . . . Especial care was taken to avoid hitting the town of St Anne roughly 600 yards behind the target . . . The spotting planes reported so many hits that on the 21st shot Captain Fitzroy (the Army Liaison Officer), remarked 'That gun bears a charmed life'. . .

As the later aerial photographs showed, the area was well and truly plastered, but unfortunately very little damage was actually done to the guns. German reports of the damage, found after the surrender, show that the cradle and recoil mechanism of one gun was damaged. Sent to Guernsey for repair two weeks later, it was some time before it was back, as a part had to be flown from Germany across liberated France. It has been suggested that the intensive AA fire kept the spotter planes at a considerable height, rendering it more difficult to assess the damage during the course of the action. At frequent intervals during the occupation period the RAF had taken stereo photograph pairs of the island. Immediately it was freed, teams were sent in who investigated the ground defences and compared them with these RAF photographs in order to positively identify the various features and assess the accuracy of their interpretation. Their report noted:

The surrender leaflet dropped by the RAF over all the Channel Islands after D-Day, August 1944

In August 1944 ROND BUT battery was shelled by HMS *Rodney* and although all the shells fell in the target area no gun was hit.

Ineffective as it proved to be in the end, this was still a remarkable feat of gunnery when one considers that the target area was approximately 170 x 140 yd, and the range about 20 miles.

Shortly after this action, on the night of 30/31 August 1944, and several more times over the next twelve nights, leaflet raids over the Channel Islands included St Anne in their coverage, and thousands of leaflets were dropped, demanding the surrender of the German forces as all communications were now cut, and food supplies stopped.

CHAPTER FIFTEEN

Capitulation

After the Allies had landed on the Normandy beaches and established their foothold in Europe on 6 June 1944, communications between the Channel Islands and France rapidly became more difficult, and, presumably to remove as much evidence as possible of their activities in the islands, especially Alderney, many of the slave workers were shipped over to St Malo. A party of slave workers and prostitutes was taken from Alderney to Guernsey on 25 June, and another on 3 July. German records show that altogether 1,222 men and 46 women were taken from Alderney to St Malo (possibly via Guernsey).

By this time Allied warships were much in evidence around the islands and some of the ships involved in these transfers were sunk on the way. By the end of the month the supply situation was beginning to get difficult for the German garrisons, and the commandant of all the German forces in the islands, Maj.-Gen. von Schmettow, notes that the lack of supplies was particularly severe on Alderney: 'Of all the islands Alderney, which had been evacuated (by the civilian population), was in the worst position'.

At this time, the garrison here was still in excess of 3,000 men, and during the winter of 1944, they had to resort to chopping up the deserted barrack huts at Sylt camp for fuel. It was during this period that much of the devastation found by the relieving forces must have occurred, when most of the unoccupied houses had their doors, windows, staircases and even roof timbers stripped out.

Towards the end of 1944 the Germans mounted an unsuccessful raid from Jersey to Granville on the nearby French coast, to try to capture some Allied supply ships. Their situation was only relieved at Christmas 1944 after negotiations with the International Red Cross, whose supply ship *Vega* then delivered food parcels for the civilians in Jersey and Guernsey, thus relieving the pressure on the food stocks for the garrison a little.

It seems never to have occurred to the Germans that the Allies, in any counter-attack on Europe that they might have mounted, would simply bypass the islands, instead of using them as a staging point. In the event, the entire defensive installations were totally wasted, and few shots were 'fired in anger', except for the bombardment of some of the Normandy beaches from Alderney.

Jersey and Guernsey were finally liberated on 9 May 1945, after Churchill had made his famous speech, '. . . and our dear Channel Islands will be relieved today. . . .'.

The liberation of these two islands is still, some forty-five years later, an occasion for a public holiday and much rejoicing each year.

Poor little Alderney had virtually no-one to liberate, and a further week was to pass before, on 16 May 1945, the British Force 135, under Brig. A.E. Snow, approached Alderney from Guernsey in an armed trawler, with two landing craft full of the support troops. Alderney pilot Nick Allen, who had been one of the last to leave the island on his way to The Casquets to destroy fuel and equipment on 23 June 1940, piloted a minesweeper into Braye Harbour the day before to clear a channel for the approaching relief force. Having done this, he became the first man to set foot back in his homeland. Brigadier Snow landed shortly after. He was met on the jetty by a party of officers led by the German commandant, Lt.-Col. Schwalm, who, when asked to surrender, is reported to have answered in one word, 'Jawohl!' – 'Yes!'

The scene which greeted them was one of devastation. The warehouses at Braye had been stripped of their woodwork; roofs, floors, doors and windows

Brig. Snow and Col. Schwalm after the surrender, inspecting a dug-in French tank used as a machine-gun post, 16 May 1945

were all gone, burnt for fuel. Many of the other houses on the island not occupied by the enemy were in a similar state, and a number had been totally destroyed to open up fields of fire for the defences. There were piles of rubble in the streets.

Englishman George Pope and Irishman Peter Doyle met Brig. Snow's party, which included another former Alderney pilot, Fred Baron, who was the pre-war Harbour-Master, and gave some details about the events of the occupation. They had stayed in the island, with their families, working for the Germans.

The surrender was signed in a German-built house at the bottom of Braye Road, used as accommodation for German naval officers, and ever since known as Peacehaven. Lt.-Col. E.G. Jones RA accepted the surrender from Lt.-Col. Schwalm, and the terms were signed at two tables, each of which now bears a brass plate commemorating the fact. The tables may now be found, one in the States Chamber where it is used by the clerk, and the other in the Alderney Museum.

Later the same day the German officers accompanied Brig. Snow on an inspection of the town and principal fortifications.

The following day, two officers and twenty men were removed from The Casquets. Six were left, temporarily, for maintenance.

On 20 May, 2,332 German prisoners, including about 175 sick and injured, were taken in five landing craft to internment in POW camps in England. This still left about 1,100 German nationals, including the civilian technicians, in the island to help with the clearing up of the mines and barbed wire, to clear the streets and to put some of the houses in order. A few of them remained permanently, especially those associated with the *Todt* workers farm, eventually married local girls and are here to this day. A few French women still remained in the island too.

The Germans surrendered their arms, dismantled the booby traps, and had already started clearing the mines. They were confined to the north-eastern part of the island, with the officers at first at Château à L'Etoc. They continued to operate the electricity plant, the cranes at the harbour, and the bakery. The town was placed out of bounds to all troops, British or German, and a temporary British HQ was set up in a ship alongside the jetty with radio communication to Guernsey.

Next day, another former pilot, Dick Allen, brother of Nick, arrived in the corvette HMS *Leith*. He had been wounded, and spent a few days here looking round and noting the damage and the fortifications.

Brig. Snow returned to Guernsey leaving Col. Jones in charge, and thus was ended the German occupation of Alderney.

German POWs being taken to the harbour *en route* for England, 17 May 1945 (Photograph courtesy of RAF Museum, London)

A few days after, Brig. Snow returned with Judge French and Col. Arnold, later Sir William Arnold, Bailiff of Guernsey. As well as the wrecked houses and the streets full of rubble, they found the church locked and in use as a storehouse. Most of the fittings had been removed and there was a German caretaker. The situation so depressed Judge French that he seriously considered abandoning Alderney for good, and not reuniting the island and its population. In a review of his findings then, written in January 1947, the Judge wrote:

My return to the island a few days after recapture was a grim experience. My first impression was of damage, destruction and devastation. Houses were broken, and the streets full of indescribable dust and rubble, weeds were everywhere.

A little later still, intelligence officer Maj. T.X.H. Pantcheff arrived from Guernsey in the RASC launch *Gamp*, on a four day visit, during which he interrogated many of the Germans and the few remaining slave workers, including a Russian major. By the time he arrived, most of the rubble had been removed from the streets, and about 15,000 of the 37,000 mines had been cleared.

At the end of May, Maj. B.E. Arnold RA arrived from Guernsey with 130 men of 'A' Battery 614 Regt. RA, and relieved the unit already here. Col. Jones had set up his HQ in Val des Portes, formerly used by the Germans as an officers' mess, and placed Maj. Arnold in charge of the German prisoners. The prisoners were still circulating freely at the north-eastern end of the island with some of the officers in *Balmoral* and *Essex House*. Maj. Arnold arrested Col. Schwalm, and took him and several other officers to the Alderney prison to await removal to Guernsey. They found the prison in a filthy state, and the Germans objected strongly, but were told they had made it so and must put up with it. The German troops were rounded up and Maj. Arnold organized them into 802 POW Camp. Most of the prisoners were housed in Fort Albert and Fort Tourgis. The British troops were billeted in Borkhum camp, the only one of the German camps left undamaged, and it was renamed Minerva camp.

The Germans were still engaged in clearing the mines, under their own officer Lt. Beck, while others were surveying and repairing the houses in town, or were employed in farming activities. Much of the furniture left behind by the departing islanders in 1940 had been looted or destroyed. What remained in the occupied houses had, in many cases, been moved to other houses for the convenience of the German garrison. This was all removed to store, in States' buildings, principally the court house and in *Balmoral*, and locked up pending the return of the islanders.

After some difficulties between Maj. Arnold and the remaining German officers and troops in Fort Albert, mainly due to language problems, RSM Willie Schröder was appointed as *Lager-Führer* to keep discipline. The officers, except for the doctor, were soon removed from Alderney. The men, now better fed than they had been of late, gave little trouble, and were allowed to organize concerts, bathing at Longis, etc., and a newspaper, *Der Tag* or the *Tourgis Times and Albert Advertiser*, was started. A second paper, *Gun-Fun or Sarnian Salvoes* was also started by the sister unit of the Alderney group, 618 Regiment RA, in Guernsey. The second issue of this latter newspaper, released in June, contained a story by the padre of the Alderney unit, of a rough trip to Guernsey in a small launch accompanied by 'The Major'.

Also at the end of May, Arthur Jennings, a former Alderney pilot who was now a captain, and Bonny Newton were sent to Alderney in two LCTs (landing craft tanks) to help in the disposal at sea of many of the mines, and much of the German ammunition. In August they were joined by two more LCTs, who brought 1,000 tons of engineering stores, two locomotives for the mineral railway and a mechanical digger, and took away scrap metal from the fortifications to Guernsey.

Sapper George Onions was killed when one of the booby trapped mines he was clearing exploded, and was buried in the churchyard on 21 June. His grave is still regularly decorated with flowers by the islanders. By the end of August most of the mines, roll bombs from the cliffs, beach tetrad defences and barbed wire had gone. The trenches across the airfield had been filled and levelled, the obstructions cleared, and the three grass runways forming a letter A, laid out by the garrison engineer, Capt. Tudor (who gave his name to part of the road at Newtown where some new houses were later erected). This pattern of runways is still retained today, although the main runway has been lengthened, tarmacked and widened since then.

Between this date and the time Judge French led the first party of returning islanders ashore from the Lt. Governor's launch, MV *Guillemot*, at 10.30 a.m. on 2 December, various legal formalities were necessary to re-establish the government of Alderney. (These, and later legislation, are detailed in chapter nineteen.) In the intervening six months much reclamation and rehabilitation work was carried out by both the army and the German prisoners.

Lt.-Gen. Sir Phillip Neame VC, KBE, CB, DSO was sworn in as Lt. Governor of Guernsey on 25 August, and immediately flew himself to Alderney to see how the work was progressing. As a result of his interest, his liaison with the Alderney Rehabilitation Committee, and the work done already under the control of Col. Power, head of the civil affairs unit in Guernsey, whom Neame immediately appointed as his government secretary, things were making good progress.

By 23 October the Mignot Memorial Hospital in Victoria Street was again ready for use. Twenty shops had been made ready, and repairs to the breakwater had been started. Gen. Neame paid another visit on 5 November accompanied by two WVS ladies, the Misses Bertram and Owen, to make arrangements for the reception of the first group of returning islanders. The arrangements made then later worked smoothly and to a strict time-table.

CHAPTER SIXTEEN

The Devastation

During the German occupation of Alderney a number of buildings were demolished to clear fields of fire for the artillery batteries, or were used as target practice. Among the more obvious of these was the Roman Catholic presbytery and several houses at Crabby Village, together with all the stout stone houses along Platte Saline, as can be seen in the aerial photograph below. The picture

The houses on Platte Saline in 1944, showing the extent of the devastation

The same row of houses as in the previous picture on Platte Saline, before the war

above shows these before the war. The stone house on Burhou was destroyed and some of the damage to Fort Hommeaux Florains was done during this period, although the greatest part of the damage now visible is the work of subsequent storms.

Many more houses were modified to provide machine-gun posts, and underground shelters and stores were built in many gardens, especially of houses in St Anne. Most of these had the name of the German who either built or was to occupy it, or the unit number, cut into the wet concrete over the entrance. Examples can still be found in a number of places.

In building the various defence positions, no regard was given to the former use or importance of the site, and good and poor agricultural land alike was undermined by a network of gun emplacements and tunnels. The shores and cliffs were similarly disfigured. A lot of land is still unusable because of the siting of defences just below the surface, rendering ploughing or machine cultivation hazardous or impossible.

The building of the two anti-tank walls, at Longis Bay and Platte Saline, has caused permanent modification to the ecology of the island. Longis Common has become a fixed sand dune and has lost the margins where changes in the vegetation were regularly noted year by year, as the varying tides and winds took

The anti-tank wall at Platte Saline in 1990

their affect. Also on Longis Common, the Neolithic dolmen *Les Porciaux* became a gun emplacement and one of the burial chambers was adapted for this purpose. It is perhaps only fair to say that the greatest damage to this part was actually caused by the attempt to remove scrap metal after the war, but the Germans removed the standing stones and one of the capstones, which had formerly been a noticeable feature of the Common, to improve the field of fire for a machine-gun battery higher up. The Hanging Rock had had about 20 ft blown off its top for the same reason.

The anti-tank wall at Platte Saline is still about 12 ft high where the stream coming down Le Vallée passes underneath it, keeping this part of the beach washed clear of accumulating sand and shingle. In the 1960s residents in the new houses along here used ladders to get down onto the beach from the road in front of their houses, but today there is rarely more than about a foot between the top of the wall and the beach level. The top of this area, above High Water Mark, is now colonized by a range of dune and shingle plants which are helping to fix the surface permanently. Storms sometimes expose the remaining iron tetrad defences.

Another of the pre-war installations demolished by the Germans in 1941 was the Cachalière Pier. One of the Granite Company's installations which had last

Tank traps on Platte Saline exposed by a storm in February 1990

been used for the export of stone about 1923, the Germans called this area *Sudehafen* (Southern Harbour), and above it was the interesting installation illustrated opposite.

When Force 135, under Brig. Snow, sailed into the island on 16 May 1945, they found scarcely a house with a roof on around the harbour, and in the other parts of the island only those houses occupied by the troops were more or less intact. During the latter days of the war, fuel had been extremely short, and anything which would burn was used.

It was some considerable time after this before the beaches, cliffs and fields were cleared of mines and other obstructions, and it became possible to expand cultivation once again, and safe for the islanders to return.

The parish church of St Anne had, despite Herzog's intervention at an early stage in the occupation, once again been turned into a store and was in a very poor state. All the pews had been ripped out and burnt, and the bells had been removed from the belfry and taken away to be melted down. Two were still on the quay, and, by good fortune, the other four were found in a field near Cherbourg after the war, identified, and eventually returned to Alderney in

Cachalière Pier being blown up by the Germans, 9 October 1941

Cachalière Pier in 1989

1946. They hung in temporary wooden frames in the churchyard and were chimed by hand until, after recasting of some, and retuning, they were returned to the belfry in 1953. They continued to be chimed until the first band of bell-ringers was started in May 1979.

All of the machinery of the quarrying industry and of the stone crusher had been removed, or damaged beyond repair. In the end, the industry, the major employer in the island before the war, was never restarted although the UK Ministry of Works did continue to quarry small amounts of stone blocks for maintaining the breakwater, for many years after the war.

CHAPTER SEVENTEEN

The Graves

Since the end of the occupation there have been a number of claims made concerning the deaths of prisoners and slaves while held in Alderney, from acts of violence by both the guards and 'kapos' as well as from starvation and disease. Stories have been told of large numbers of bodies being dumped off the breakwater, until senior German officers complained about the pollution of Braye Bay and the practice was stopped. Many sick workers are reputed to have been pushed off the cliffs at Fort Albert, sometimes after being shot.

Tales have also been told about workers being pushed into the wet concrete as various defence works were being constructed. This, at least, seems unlikely since the presence of pockets of organic matter within the structure would seriously weaken its strength, and the 'fortress grade' works were part of the scheme to help the Third Reich last 1,000 years. There are, however, two reported occasions, by apparently reliable witnesses, of groups of about a dozen bodies being buried in shallow pits on the beach in front of the wall at Longis, at very low spring tides. There are no reports of bodies becoming exposed in subsequent storms, however.

Examining the reports and photographs of German troops, and even the 'Daily Orders' issued to the garrison in Fort Tourgis and the Christmas ration schedules, already quoted, it can be seen that at least a part of the work was done by the Germans themselves. Paid volunteer OT workers, often only here for short periods for a specific job and generally better treated and fed than the slaves, were also used.

If we can accept the several reports of sick workers being taken back to the mainland of Europe for 'disposal', and the records of the court martial of Max List and Kurt Klebeck confirm at least one shipment of 200 or so prisoners, then it must also be accepted that many of these deaths did not actually take place in Alderney, and there is therefore no record of them in the island. This, of course, does not make those responsible for the condition of the prisoners and slave workers any less culpable in the final result, but other reports have established that at least some of those victims were rested and rehabilitated before being set to other work.

One at least of the tales was proven shortly after the freeing of the island, when the rumoured 'false-bottomed coffin' was found among the Russian graves in the long grass on Longis Common. When the remains from here were exhumed for repatriation, however, only a very few graves contained more than one corpse, suggesting that it was used for economy and to preserve the appearance of a civilized burial rather than to disguise multiple deaths, although the coffin was actually large enough to contain two bodies.

The difficulties experienced by the occupying forces in transporting men and materials in safety after the British naval forces began to patrol the area around the islands in 1942, would suggest that to needlessly dispose of workers did not make sense. However, the actions of the Nazis, and especially the 'Death's-head' Brigade SS elsewhere in Europe, certainly point to a lack of concern for sensible and economic use of human resources. The high degree of uncivilized behaviour in many of the members of this group, and of the camp 'kapos' or 'trusties', well documented and proved in other camps, seems quite likely to have been continued here in Alderney.

Maj. Pantcheff found almost up-to-date records, although he found them confusing, sometimes misleading and, according to prisoners still on the island, incomplete. However, they were detailed (if not always truthful) in their

A grave on Longis Common, 1945

content, and matched many of the marked graves found. A chart was prepared of the recorded burials. A total of sixty-four graves, containing only sixty bodies, were found in St Anne's churchyard, mostly in the north-west corner just beyond the church itself. Of these, forty-five were of Russians. Almost all of these deaths took place between the end of September and the middle of November 1942. A chart, kept in the States Offices, shows their position.

On Longis Common there were 319 named graves, containing 326 bodies, and another chart was prepared of these. Again the graves were mostly of Russians, including forty-three unknown Russian citizens, with eight named graves of French Jews nearby. There were thus 437 bodies found in marked graves. Since the OT firm 'employing' the workers had to pay for their funeral costs it is at least probable that some others were buried where they fell.

The German Cemetery at Valongis, just off the Longis road, contained sixty-one graves, eleven of them from the sinking of *Hermann* and *Schleswig Holstein* in February 1942. Maj. Pantcheff noted that during the peak period of slave-

The memorial stone put up in the
German Cemetery by the POWs in 1946

worker deaths at the end of 1942, no member of the German garrison died. A total of twenty members of the garrison, which numbered up to 4–5,000 troops, died in the two and a half years covered by the recorded deaths of 389 workers.

At a later date in the 1960s, after Alderney was resettled, all of the German and foreign workers' bodies were removed from the island and reburied, an exercise carried out by the German War Graves Commission.

The memorial stone from the German Cemetery was put over the wall into the Stranger's Cemetery, the *Cimitière St Michel*, in Longis Road where it remains today. The inscription is still legible, and wrongly attributed to St John 14: 20 instead of 14: 19:

> I live and ye shall live also. Our dead comrades! German prisoners-of-war in Alderney.

The smaller size of the last line of the inscription on the 1946 photograph on p.129, is because this was erected by the German POWs after the surrender.

The memorial plaque placed on the north wall of St Anne's church before the bodies were removed

Later a plaque was placed on the north outside wall of the church where the sixty graves had been situated, and the Hammond family erected a memorial, overlooking the ground where many had been buried, to all of the prisoners of the Third Reich who had died in Alderney during the war. Annual services are held at this memorial by both Russian and French representatives to commemorate the date of the freeing of the island. On the 25th, 30th and 40th anniversaries of the liberation, a large combined service was held with former prisoners from all over Europe returning to honour their dead compatriots.

The French ex-prisoners formed an organization shortly after the war, *Les Amicales des Anciens Déportées*, and have been regular attenders with their families. Sadly, their numbers are now few. The president of this organization, M. Albert Eblagon, is now over 90, and at the 1992 ceremony only four of the former prisoners were able to attend.

CHAPTER EIGHTEEN

The Legacy

Aerial photographs taken after the war show the island of Alderney to be almost completely covered with defence installations of one sort or another. A map of the island, prepared for the invasion and marked 'secret', also highlights the amount of building carried out. Despite this general desecration of Alderney as a quiet, peaceful, rural and agricultural community, however, the Germans did leave a legacy of improved facilities which were of benefit to the returning islanders from December 1945.

Before the war most houses either had their own wells or pumps, which by all accounts were sometimes affected by drought conditions. Failing that, people had to use the public pumps in Marais Square, Sauchet Lane, in Le Vallée at the bottom of Stoney Lane, or one of the other four, all of which had year round supplies of good water. (Le Vallée was originally named after the Le Vallée family, and is not a misuse of the gender.)

The Victorian engineers who built the forts had included large collecting tanks for rain-water under the courtyards in the larger forts, but in addition, pumping stations had been installed which supplied Fort Albert and Château à L'Etoc from Corblets Quarry, and Fort Tourgis from below the Mill leat in Val de la Bonne Terre. These may have been extended somewhat, and there was a piped water system installed in much of the town area. The Germans supplied this from the high level tank on top of the tower at Le Mouriaux. A permanent and highly visible reminder of the occupation, it now forms a valuable part of the island water system, and there is also a facility attached to enable farmers to fill tankers rapidly, for watering their cattle in the fields. There was another four-storied tower (the tactical HQ known as Hoffmannshöhe) on the present site of the Telephone Exchange which was demolished to make way for the aerial mast when this was built.

The main water collection tank installed by the Germans at the top of the Alles ès Fées was filled with water originating at the springs by the airport, now inside a bunker, and then pumped up from the reservoir below Rose Farm. It was deepened after the war by the States Water Board and covered over. It now forms a substantial reservoir and distribution point for the island supply.

The pump in Marais Square, 1946

The electricity system in the island, started by the Alderney Light and Power Company in 1936, supplied about one quarter of the houses in town. The other, erected by the granite works to provide power for the crusher, and built just behind it in 1938, was restricted in its distribution to some domestic customers in the Braye and Crabby areas. The Germans later installed a more powerful generating station here, behind the stone crusher, which continued in use until the present station was built in 1952, 100 yd away, at the side of York Hill Quarry. The building which housed the German station is in use today as the offices and storage facility of the recently set up 'Alderney Fuel Supplies'. Two of the tanks appear on a 1944 aerial photograph, and may even be the same ones.

Another generating station was built in the Water Lanes not long before the war ended. It was powered by steam, with a cooling water pool built higher up the lane. Owing to the poor quality of the lubricating oils this engine ran its bearings after only about two weeks use. They were sent to Cherbourg to be remetalled, but had not returned when the war ended, and the station was only used as a switching point for the town supply from the harbour generating station. The fitting-out of this station was completed after the war using two lend-lease American generators intended for shipment to Russia which were bought in England. The station continued in use until the York Hill Quarry station was opened in 1952. The building was finally demolished in 1973.

At the time of the surrender the total capacity was about to be increased by the addition of five generators which were still in their packing cases. These were apparently claimed by the French and sent back to France. Mains electricity was supplied all round the town, at least to the buildings in use by the occupying forces, the newly-installed telephone system and the command posts, although, as Herzog has reported, supplies were sometimes restricted by lack of diesel fuel for the generators. Other generators were situated at The Arsenal, in the pre-war station on La Hêche (converted to supply a.c.), and at The Giffoine. The overhead distribution cable network for the 10,500 volt HT supply which was set up, forms the basis of the power supply layout today, and some of the wiring was still in use in the late 1970s. It has all been replaced since, and recently much of the wiring has been placed underground. There were also a number of mobile generating sets in use to supply the power needed for some gun batteries and the high-powered radio transmitters found in good working order when the island was relieved, and capable of transmitting direct to Berlin.

Before the war the principal utility was the gas works; piped gas was available throughout St Anne, and streets and homes were lit by it. This was not used at all during the occupation. It was revived for some time afterwards, but with the extension of the electricity system, and its use for lighting in every home, the use of gas proved uneconomic and ceased to function, bottled gas being then supplied for cooking. The gas works is now the Harbour Lights Hotel, and the base of the gas-holder is now the hotel bar.

The sewerage system (which existed pre-war) was improved and extended by the Germans in the town area, using labour brought from Guernsey.

Also before the war, after the final failure of the undersea telegraph link with Guernsey and England, the principal method of communication outside the island had been the radio telegraph maintained at the post office, then in Victoria Street in the building at present occupied by Riduna Stores, and there was a small manual telephone exchange, now preserved in the museum. The transmitter was on Essex Hill.

At the time of the evacuation, the recently appointed sub-postmaster was Mr R.P. Bury. The post office was open to the public from 9 a.m. to 7 p.m. but the wireless telegraph was on 24-hour watch. At this time the Machine-Gun Corps training centre was on the island with a large contingent, removed barely a week before the occupation of the Channel Islands in order to defend the airfields at Jersey and Guernsey against possible parachutists' attacks. There was a direct telephone link from the post office to the Army HQ to relay messages.

Mr Bury finally smashed all the equipment and collected the cash and documents a few minutes before the island was evacuated on 23 June. He did not leave with the party for England on the Navy ships, but, conceiving it his duty to deliver the cash and documents to his superiors in Guernsey, persuaded the fishermen, Arthur Jennings, father and son, to take him to Guernsey where they arrived at 6 o'clock that evening.

The widespread German telephone system once again formed the basis of the first post-war installations, but these were not linked to the mainland for about eighteen months.

There were other objects and constructions, both large and small, in evidence. Some, such as the 30,317 mines, had to be dealt with before it was safe for civilians to return. The Germans had left carefully prepared maps of the distribution of these, but there were a number of booby traps to catch the unwary, such as a second mine planted below the first, which went off when the disabled mine was removed. A number of German prisoners, set to the task of clearing these, were reported killed, as, unfortunately, was one of the British bomb disposal team, Sapper George Onions. In addition, numbers of Roll Bombs were found on the cliffs. Even now, forty-five years later, more turn up from time to time below the cliffs. A 500 lb bomb was found in Corblets Quarry in 1989. As work progressed care had to be taken in exploding all items removed, as the shock waves, travelling through the bedrock caused damage to properties in town.

There was also a burnt-out German dredger in Little Crabby Harbour, which had to be removed, the wreck of *Staffa* by the entrance to the inner harbour, and *VP 703* and *Henny Fricke* in the middle of Braye Bay.

On the positive side, and of future benefit to the islanders, a number of roadways were improved. Most noticeable was the concrete roadway, much of it over the line of the old rough track from Whitegates to Braye Harbour (the present 'Lower Road'), continuing on round Crabby Bay, and with an entirely new section between Picaterre Farm and the sea, along Platte Saline to the bottom of Le Petit Val and on to Fort Tourgis. The present road from the lighthouse to Longis is also an entirely German construction, the pre-war unmetalled road still running along the shore line.

Another construction was the causeway to Fort Clonque, allowing vehicular access to the fort. Built by the Germans towards the end of 1942, it was badly breached at one spot and repaired in the 1970s. It was again in need of a certain amount of small repairs, carried out in 1990, when mains water and electricity

A derelict German dredger in New Harbour, 1945

A former German hut, re-erected and transformed into a house at Quesnard

were taken to the fort. It is still in regular use today, both by walkers and by the Landmark Trust workers, who come in parties of a dozen or so throughout the summer season for a holiday.

The causeway to Raz Island and its fort was strengthened, and is still in regular use for the residents in the fort and also, until quite recently, for the visitors to the small Sea Bird Museum and the restaurant established there. The fort has now reverted to a private dwelling. They still have their own generator for electricity, a modern replacement for the one installed by the Germans. Both of these causeways provide access at most states of the tide, although that to Raz is flooded at every high tide, and to Clonque at high spring tides.

The sectional jetty already described was in use for many years after the war, although the three large cranes erected on it by the Germans were deemed to be too large for the needs of Alderney, and removed. The jetty continued in use until about 1970, by which time, through lack of suitable maintenance, the iron structure was beginning to rot. The planking was taken up and the jetty fell into disuse. After much discussion it was finally demolished in 1978, repair by then being too costly, although its demolition, too, was at considerable expense to the States. The demolition was inefficiently carried out and some of the base sections left constituted a hazard to shipping, resulting in later additional expense to the States when the fragments had to be removed in the 1980s.

The electric German bakery set up just below Victoria Street in the wooded area of Le Vallée, is still in use today as the island bakery. The slaughter house in Le Val was converted many years ago to use as the States' dairy, recently modernized it is still in use.

At the time of the surrender some of the slave camps had already been broken up and destroyed, but many huts remained in various parts of the island, and Borkhum was still intact. It was taken over by the British garrison, and renamed Minerva. Some time later, after the British forces were withdrawn, the remaining huts were offered to the islanders, in the *Billet D'Etat* for 23 March 1946, at a price between 2d. minimum and 6d. maximum per superficial foot. Some sold for as little as 10s. (50p) and were re-erected in various parts of the island to make homes, sheds, farm buildings or workshops.

A former German convalescent hut in Essex Valley, now turned into a house

Several of the German buildings thus moved are still to be seen, including a delightful shingle-hung bungalow near the lighthouse, with an interesting wall mural of fishes made from ormer and scallop shells, erected on the site of a row of cottages demolished by the Germans and the commandant's bungalow from Sylt on Longis Common, to which reference has already been made. There is another small building on the site next door.

Some more permanent concrete barrack buildings were erected, and are still in use. The German farm at the old brickfields provides a pleasant house now called Pasadena and there are two similar houses in Barrackmaster's Lane which were formerly used as sick quarters or convalescent homes for German officers. The owner of one has developed the most beautiful garden in this sheltered valley.

Many houses still use the bunkers built in their gardens as stores, cellars and workshops, and a number of properties have been constructed incorporating them into the structure. One such can be seen behind Picaterre Farm, and another, with the inscription 'Enders Bunker 1944', is at the junction of Little Street and La Marette.

One of the three 1942 German paintings on the ceiling at 45 High Street. The paintings were removed in 1946

Some homes, and a few bunkers, had been decorated with murals by the occupying troops, and in a house at 45 High Street, three panels of ceiling paintings were found. These were removed carefully and two of them, cleaned and restored, now hang in the museum.

On Platte Saline, the stone gate pillars of Helgoland camp, and the concrete entrance area where the guardhouse stood, now form the forecourt of a charming bungalow, Quatrième. A second pair of pillars, somewhat reduced in height, can still be seen further along the road close to the remains of the former boiler house and laundry, now incorporated into a private garage. Inside the garage of another house in Le Petit Val, one of the water collecting or storage tanks of the camp has been incorporated as an inspection pit. The water supply tanks, channelling the stream which runs down from Ladysmith, are still to be found in one garden, and the foundations and underground sewage tanks of the camp lavatory block are still in the garden next door to this.

Standing on Platte Saline itself, on the rim of the former sand pit, is a pair of parallel walls, which have defied a neighbour's attempts at demolition. The walls formed a loading bay for sand, held in hoppers which was then transferred onto trucks and lorries, run between the walls, and used for the massive concrete constructions in the island. It has been calculated that some 86,000 cubic metres of concrete in total were poured in Alderney during the war, and two excavators were kept running 24 hours a day in the sand pit below these walls.

At various times since the war many of the gun emplacements and lookout posts have been used by the people as weekend or leisure accommodation, but the lack of water, electricity and sewerage facilities at these have finally stopped this practice.

The Rink, the island cinema at the junction of High Street and Le Val, was turned into a luxury cinema by the Germans and the equipment installed continued to be used for many years after the war. A former skating rink, built originally as a Scottish presbyterian chapel for the garrison, the cinema was more recently known as The Lyceum, and in pre-war days had been a bit primitive. It eventually ceased to be used and was finally demolished in 1976 after standing empty for several years. A small portion of the western end was retained and incorporated into Lyceum House which now occupies the site.

With hindsight many of the German defence installations, which were completely intact at the time of the surrender, could have been preserved as tourist attractions. Although none are on the scale of the German underground hospital in Jersey, which now attracts many thousands of visitors each year, there were plenty that would have been of interest.

The main German hospital, off Longis Road, is still in use as the HQ of the island's Junior Militia and as the island's civil emergencies bunker. The original German radio mast is still in position.

The main German hospital off Longis Road in 1989

   Quite understandably, the returning islanders were anxious to remove from
sight as quickly as possible those reminders of the people and events which had
caused the desecration of their homes and land. Much of the concrete was so
thick and well reinforced that attempts to blow it up, or break it up, failed and
were largely abandoned. All that could be done was to remove the guns,
searchlights, range-finders and radar equipment, much of which was taken out
to sea and dumped in the Hurd Deep. Heavy equipment was removed by the
military in 1946, and scrap dealers moved in, in the 1950s, and removed most of
the doors, metal shutters, and remaining equipment from them. A few people
made a lot of money from this activity. Soil was eventually pushed over some of
the remainder, and in course of time the natural and unchecked growth of
brambles and bracken has obscured much of the rest. Still visible on the skyline
from most parts of the island is the German artillery control tower above the
quarry rim at Mannez. The islanders have come to accept its presence, and for
many years it has been referred to locally as The Odeon, after a well-known
chain of cinemas, many built just before the war in reinforced concrete, and
with similar rounded corners.

At this time no-one could have envisaged the interest that would be shown, in later years, in this dark period of the history of the world; an interest perhaps understandable, coming from British and Continental visitors of the pre-war generation, but which, more surprisingly, also comes from today's youth. Unfortunately, over forty-five years later, neither the original equipment, nor the money to purchase similar items and re-install them can be found, which would allow the control tower or other installations to be reinstated.

In the Alderney Museum, the greatest interest shown by visitors is generally to the cases containing the relics of the German occupation. In particular to the poor relics of the slave camps, a pair of the blue and white striped 'pyjamas' and some wooden clogs, found under some floorboards in Fort Albert long after the war, doubtless hidden by a German soldier to take home as a souvenir, the leather whip of one of the SS guards and other such relics.

Literature and information leaflets on this period are high on the list of purchases by visitors throughout the Channel Islands, confirming the interest shown in the various museums and installations, by visitors from all over the world. A somewhat less attractive aspect of this interest is to hear the island of Alderney being referred to by German visitors as a 'conquered part of England'. 'Conquered' scarcely seems the right word when one considers that it was an island with only seven inhabitants!

A view of the fortifications on Mannez Hill in 1990

CHAPTER NINETEEN

The Islanders Return

As recorded in chapter fifteen, the first islander to set foot on Alderney after the general surrender of the German forces in the Channel Islands, was pre-war pilot, Nick Allen. Allen had piloted the minesweeper which cleared the channel into Braye Harbour almost a week later, on 15 May, ready for the arrival of the unit of Force 135 under Brig. Alfred Snow. Snow arrived in an armed trawler, with two landing craft full of the support troops, to accept the surrender of Alderney on 16 May 1945.

It was nearly seven months before Judge French's small advance party arrived on 2 December. Included in the party were: Mrs Richards, Brig. Cosby, Lt. and Mrs Vic Carter, Mrs Riou, Mrs P. Forsyth, Mrs Martyn, Mr and Mrs Després, Mr and Mrs Osborne, and the two WVS ladies (see chapter fifteen).

Two more parties arrived on MV *Guillemot* on 4 and 6 December comprising: Capt. Richards, Mr and Mrs Dick Allen, Mr and Mrs George Jennings, Mr and Mrs Tom Herivel, Mr and Mrs John Mignot, Mr and Mrs Archie Rowe, Mr Slade, Mrs Arthur Jennings, (mostly Jurats and *Douzaine* members and their wives), Mr Gissing, sent by the Home Office to supervise the communal farm, and a further WVS detachment. The members of the parties were fed communally, twice a day, at the convent, by the WVS ladies. From here they were also issued with essential equipment – buckets, brooms, bedding, etc.– while the prisoners carried the free, mostly plywood, government issue furniture etc. for them from the central store to their own houses, or the places they were occupying until their own homes were fit to use.

A much larger party of 110 islanders arrived on the Southern Railway's SS *Autocarrier* at 8 a.m. on Saturday 15 December 1945, and was welcomed by a shower of Verey lights, an archway bearing the huge sign 'Welcome Home', a guard of honour headed by Gen. Neame, and the Guernsey Salvation Army Band which played 'Home, Sweet Home' as the ship approached with her escort of two naval launches. A speech of welcome was made by the general, the band played the National Anthem as the first passengers stepped ashore to a twenty-one round salute from the rifles of the soldiers, and Guernseyman Mr C.A. Pritchard, divisional marine manager of the Southern Railway at Southampton, read another speech of welcome on behalf of the railway

Mrs Bessie Duplain disembarking from SS *Autocarrier* returning to Alderney, December 1946

company who had transported them. Forty years later, the anniversary of this event was commemorated by the manufacture of a bronze lapel badge bearing a representation of the ship, and the date. The badge is regularly worn with pride by those islanders, the 'Boat People', who returned at that time. Two more parties arrived in *Autocarrier* on 22 and 28 December, making a total of 360 islanders now back in their homeland.

The returning islanders were taken to reception centres at the Grand Hotel and the Belle Vue Hotel, run by the WVS, where they were housed until they returned to their own homes, carrying the bare necessities issued from the communal store. Meals continued to be provided twice a day at the convent as many houses were without a stove. *Autocarrier* also continued to provide a weekly run from Southampton with baggage, furniture and fresh foodstuffs for some time.

The pre-war civilian administration was liaising closely with the military immediately following their return, while trying to set up their own organization. For the time being, the States' Chamber having been stripped of most of its woodwork and fittings by the Germans, and also being full of the impounded furniture, States' Meetings were held in the schoolroom on Saturday afternoons, and the People's Meetings were held in the cinema. The Judge had leased Val des Portes from the Kay-Mouat family, and set up his administrative offices in the German huts built in the grounds, where he is said to have had the island's only working telephone, with an extension to the airways office.

At this period the People's Meetings proposed and voted on various matters of common interest, which the Judge then placed before the States, with his own proposals. At the beginning of March 1946, the people, urged on by People's Deputy William Herivel, proprietor of the Marais Hall, had proposed, and voted unanimously for, a change in the way the money in the Resettlement Accounts was administered and the setting up of a committee to supervise it. The only tax currently being levied was the *Impôt* duty, no property taxes having been assessed, and the Judge also proposed in the *Billet* for the March States' Meeting, either that a committee should be set up to control the finances which, as he said, would have to sit continuously, or that one of several alternatives should be adopted, and that the *Douzaine* should be asked to assess each item of real property for taxation, to raise revenue. The committee idea was rejected at the States' Meeting, and he remained in control of the finances.

A second meeting was held in March, attended by the Lt. Governor, at which the disposal of the German huts (already mentioned) was proposed, and also the disposal of the £9,406 18s. 0½d. remaining from the proceeds of the sale of the cattle and other items officially removed by the Guernsey parties in June 1940 which was then being returned. The Guernsey authorities had deducted some £2,300 for their expenses in relation to the salvage operation, plus their expenses in selling the animals, and had retained the rest in an Alderney salvage account, without adding any interest, throughout the intervening period. Much to the further discontent of the States' Members, the Judge decreed that this money was to be placed in the farm account against the debt to Britain, and not used for the good of the community. Although it really belonged to the individuals whose property had been sold, it was impossible to ascertain who should benefit by what amounts, as no individual records of the sales had been kept.

It was noted in the *Billet* that the British troops were to be withdrawn on 1 June, and the Judge proposed that the States must prepare a budget for the remainder of 1946 within a month. The April 1946 *Billet* was concerned with re-establishing communications, running the harbour, and setting up various committees to run the island.

Proposals were received in December, from Mr Ford of the British Channel Island Shipping Co. in Guernsey, to establish a shipping service between Guernsey and Alderney. The service would provide a 90 ft vessel for transporting goods, and another vessel capable of carrying some 300 passengers, a service hitherto catered for by the military with the LCT captained by Arthur Jennings. The company's terms stated that they be given a monopoly, that no Alderney boat be so employed, and that if they made a loss in the first year, harbour dues and pilotage would be remitted. A proposal was also received from the Great Western Railway to re-establish a direct link with Weymouth, provided that all harbour dues and pilot's fees were paid by the States for the first six months.

Of the cranes which had been left at the harbour by the Germans, two, one German, the other Czech, were handed over to the States, and two of the farm workers were to be trained to replace the German drivers. These cranes would be the responsibility of the Roads Committee, and the drivers would be paid out of States' revenue and not from the farm account.

The more important of the pre-war committees were brought back, at least temporarily, with their original members, and any other people with suitable experience could be co-opted to assist. A fuel controller (C.G. Kay-Mouat) was appointed, and various committees set up – the Resettlement Stocks Issue Committee, with one States' Member, to control the issue of the government furniture and the redistribution to their original owners of items which had remained and been placed in store by the military, and another to control repatriation and employment.

The May *Billet* contained the budget for the remainder of 1946, and proposals for raising direct taxation on property, which simply amounted to a revival of the *Besoin Publique* at an increased level to raise an extra £1,000. The members declined to institute any other taxes despite the judge's efforts to persuade them. The budget gave details of the anticipated expenditure of the various committees. These, by then, included: education, roads, lighting, building, sanitation, plantations, and publicity. The annual wages of the principal employees were noted: Inspector of Explosives, £30; *Procureur du Roi*, £50; Treasurer's Clerk, £20; HM Sergeant, £15; HM Sheriff, £1; Police Officer, £156; *Impôt* Receiver, £66 10s.

A request was also received in November from Mr H.A. Paine, owner of the Alderney Gravel and Grit Company which he had started in 1936 on Platte Saline beach, to restart operations, despite the fact that the gravel washing machinery he had designed had disappeared. Mr Paine proposed to lay on a supply of fresh water to wash the gravel, from one of the streams discharging onto Platte Saline, by piping it to the fort. He anticipated giving employment to nine men and a boy. There was also a request for the somewhat belated payment of a bill for £264 19s. 2d. (dated 8 August 1938) from a, by-then deceased, Guernsey engineer, which was for work carried out in designing a water and sewage scheme for Alderney. The scheme was to have cost £13,915, but was never carried out.

A communal food shop had been established in Victoria Street in the premises now occupied by Bell's Estate Agency, potatoes from the crop planted by the Germans were on sale. The post office was functioning where Riduna Stores is now situated. Capt. Richards had re-opened his newsagent and tobacconist shop, surprisingly finding the pre-war stock where he had hidden it. The shop still occupies the same premises at the junction of Victoria and Ollivier Streets. The airport had been re-opened on 15 February with the first commercial flight, a chartered DH Rapide from Liverpool, whose passengers were Bert Hammond and his father from the Campania Inn. The Channel Island Airways office was again open at what is now Colenso House. The GWR had actually restarted a weekly service from Weymouth with SS *Roebuck* on 25 March, by arrangement with Judge French, before the terms had been agreed in the States.

A new vicar, Revd E.P. St John from Guernsey, a former RAF chaplain, had taken up residence in April, and the Campania, the Rose and Crown, Marais Hall, and the Billiards Inn were all functioning again.

A qualified nurse, Mrs Reg Duplain, had started the school again, assisted by Mrs Chris Simon and 13-year-old Miriam Angel, who took the infants, as the children were running wild and getting into danger in the bunkers. They were paid £1 a week each.

With the withdrawal of the troops due in a week or two's time, the islanders would then become totally dependent on themselves and their own resources to survive. The last of the German prisoners were withdrawn on 1 June, and before they left they gave a concert in The Lyceum (cinema) to culminate the various concerts and dances provided by their orchestra under the baton of one of the prisoners, a well-known pre-war conductor named Stimmler. The army finally withdrew at the end of the month.

The discontent, however, was growing in a population whose activities were primarily limited to the communal farm, and it had already led to the builders and craftsmen being released from the fields to work at their own trades, at pre-war piece-work rates, on the communal building schemes, assisted by German prisoners. This differential in pay, of course, gave further cause for discontent. In April, the privately-owned furniture was still locked up, and issue furniture was still in good supply for those returning. Judge French had set up a Resettlement Stocks Issue Committee of four people, with Brigadier Cosby in charge of the war booty furniture stocks. The islanders, not unnaturally, did not agree that their cherished possessions were to be classified as 'war booty', and could be issued to people making claims for an article of similar description, and a great deal of discontent arose when some items were found in neighbour's houses.

The extended terms of office of the pre-war members of the legislature were due to expire on 30 September 1946 and elections should have been arranged.

As yet there was no electoral roll and no taxes were being paid. The Judge was in favour of elections (which he presumably hoped would get rid of Billy Herivel who was constantly challenging his actions), but when the States voted against them by a single vote majority, after the court had tied on their vote, the Judge refused to accept the decision and made certain threats about the effect on relations with the Home Office. Despite these threats, no elections were held.

Gen. Neame was greatly concerned at the situation in Alderney and came over every two or three weeks in 1946. His concern was shared by the Home Office, and an enquiry was set up, to which the people were invited, which convened in Alderney on 28 September.

The Judge called another People's Meeting at The Lyceum on 22 October, at which, in an eight point agenda, he proposed to put the current situation before the people with regard to houses and furniture, land ownership, employment prospects, States' services including the electricity supply, transport, finances, and the island administration.

The situation of the people, with food, clothing, fuel and petrol still rationed, bad communications, no outside telephones, and an unreliable electricity supply, was not helped by the unusually harsh winter of 1946/7. There was thick snow, and water froze; at one stage, the farm horses broke out from their quarters near Essex Castle and came into town looking for water. The land boundaries had not yet been settled by the *Douzaine*; the German huts had not, in many cases, been removed by their purchasers within the required three months, from their original sites where they were no longer wanted. Other examples of procrastination were lampooned by Ian Glasgow in his revived *Island Review*. This publication had been restarted when Glasgow found his pre-war printing machine in Guernsey and brought it back. He operated from the building in Longis Road just beyond the present telephone exchange.

In March 1947 Gen. Neame told the States of the British Government's decision to disband the communal farm at the end of the year, and this was followed by a Home Office letter, dated 21 June 1947 and headlined in the *Guernsey Press* as 'Great Britain's Ultimatum to Alderney'.

The result of all the dissension was the setting up of a Home Office enquiry, and the drafting of *The Government of Alderney Law, 1948*.

The States' Meetings were held from July 1947 in the old Militia Arsenal in Ollivier Street, and finally the question of the private furniture still stored in the States' Chamber was settled during that summer, when it was laid out at various times on The Butes in fine weather, tables etc. one week, wardrobes and beds another, and so on. People were allowed to examine it and decide which items were theirs. They then lined up at the opposite end of The Butes, and when a whistle was blown ran for the furniture and had to place a hand on the items

The 'Battle of the Butes', 1946

they claimed. These 'Battles of The Butes' were the final downfall of the Judge's administration, his candidates for the two vacancies on the Jurats' bench failed to get elected, and when the commissioners arrived on 15 September, the islanders laid many accusations about his conduct before them.

Judge French, who had almost single-handedly, if somewhat autocratically, guided the affairs of his beloved island since before the war, resigned and retired to the seclusion of his house. He died in 1962, while on a visit to South Africa. He had erected a marble memorial tablet to his wife in Lincoln Cathedral, of which he had been a benefactor, and to it was added his name.

CHAPTER TWENTY

The Return Legislation

POST SECOND WORLD WAR

In March 1945, while Alderney was still occupied by the enemy, a deputation of leading citizens attended the Home Office, and announced the wish of the majority of islanders to return home when hostilities ceased. They were told that if it were possible that the island could be economically independent, the British Government would offer financial and other assistance to enable them to do so.

The island was re-occupied by British forces on 16 May 1945, and on 11 August 1945 a Committee of Enquiry was set up by the Home Secretary under the Lt. Governor of Guernsey, Lt.-Gen. Sir Philip Neame, to decide on the resettlement of Alderney. The committee visited the island, and, back in London, held a meeting with the surviving members of the States of Alderney, the Alderney Relief Committee, and a few other islanders. The result of this meeting was a short document with six recommendations, summarized as follows:

1. The first task is to bring the land back into cultivation and replace boundary markers. For a year, or two cropping seasons, the entire island will be farmed as a single unit and no rent will be paid to the land-owners.

2. The only form of employment in the first stage will be under the farm manager. Rates of pay: men, £3 a week; women, 1s. per hour; juveniles, 9d. per hour. Shopkeepers will be provided with shop-fittings and an initial stock, after which they will replace the goods from their sales, and the work done by skilled craftsmen, employed by any resident, will be paid for by the employer.

Some people of independent means may be allowed to return. This will be limited by the availability of food and housing. The school is being made ready, and equipped. The steamer service will be limited and restricted, visitors will not be allowed, and the islanders will have to stay there for some time.

3. Population will return by groups, as conditions allow.

4. After normal conditions on the land have been restored, the farmers and land-owners will decide how to continue.

5. The military have made over 300 houses habitable. As far as possible people can return to their own houses and shops. All furniture and equipment left in the island has been placed in a communal store and will be allocated. Some essential furniture will be sent from England, and issued free.

6. The attached application form to return, should be filled in and returned to the home office by 23 November 1945.

This document was sent to all of the Alderney exiles in the UK.

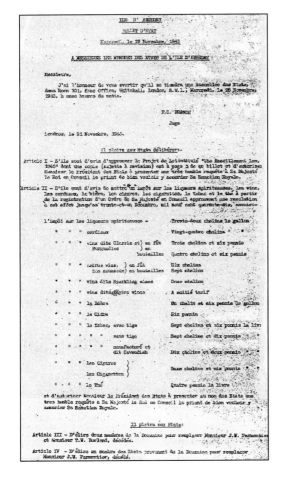

The *Billet d'Etat* for the only meeting of a Channel Island States ever held outside the islands, 26 November 1945

An order-in-council, dated 16 November 1945, had established the initial government of the island in the hands of those who had been members of the States at the time of the evacuation, with Judge F.G. French still at the head, and on 28 November 1945, the Judge held a meeting of the States at the Home Office. This is the first, and only, time in history when a meeting of the States of any Channel Island has been held outside the island. It was preceeded by a short meeting of the *Douzaine*. The *Billet D'Etat* (still written in both French and English at this time, with the content decided by the Judge) for the States' Meeting contained:

1. the draft of the Resettlement Law 1945, which empowered the measures necessary to effect item 1. above, which, in turn, received the Royal assent on 20 December, and which was to remain in force until 31 December 1947;

2. suggestions for the various *Impôt* duties which were to be levied on alcohol, tobacco and tea, until 31 December 1946. These included: spirits, 32s. a gallon; wines averaged about 5s. a gallon; Beer, 1s. 6d.a gallon; cigarettes, 11s. 6d. a pound; and tea, 4d. a pound;

3. recommendations to elect one member of the *Douzaine* to the States to replace a dead member, and two new members of the *Douzaine*.

As recorded above, Judge French, still head of the island administration but now also a brigadier-general (a title he stopped using as soon as he was back home), was the first of the official returnees to step ashore on Sunday 2 December 1945, followed by the advance party of a dozen or so. They were followed over the next four days by two more small groups which included Naval Capt. Charles Richards and the Jurats and *Douzaine*, many of whom now held military field-ranks. The Southern Railway car ferry *Autocarrier* arrived on 15 December with another 110 islanders, and she brought two more groups to make up about 360 people by the end of 1945.

Up to the war four different types of taxes had been levied in Alderney. The *Besoin Publique* was a tax paid solely by those property owners who constituted the Electorate (which at this time still excluded publicans, Roman Catholics, and married women, as had been the pre-war status), the qualification for which was the possession of real (i.e. land and buildings) property worth more than 5 quarters of wheat rent, taken as worth £100. At the same time there had been a requirement for jurats to hold property worth 20 quarters of wheat rent, i.e. about £400. The Poor Law tax was used for the support of the needy, young and old, and was similarly levied. The Road Tax was levied only on land-owners whose property actually fronted on to a public road, and brought in about £38 a year. Finally, there was the *Impôt* or duty paid on alcohol etc. There was no income tax.

By the end of July 1946 there were about 150 persons in the first tax-paying category (the *Besoin Publique*) back in Alderney, out of a total of 685 people who had so far returned (about half the pre-war population). The dissension which developed in the middle of 1946 between the Judge and the islanders was partly due to their enforced living and working in a sort of commune, with a standard rate of pay and with little say in the work they were to do, or control over their former property or the profits of their labours, and partly because of personality clashes between the judge and some of the islanders. It was also, no doubt, caused by the different attitudes which had developed by virtue of the islanders' experiences in a far greater world than their own small realm, during the previous five to six years.

The profits from the people's work had been administered personally by the Judge and put into two resettlement accounts, a general and a farm account, to repay the debt for the money expended on rehabilitation and repairs, as had been decreed by the British Government in the resettlement plans.

The concern of both the Lt. Governor, Sir Philip Neame, and the Bailiff, Ambrose Sherwill CBE, MC (later to become Sir Ambrose), in Guernsey, and also of the British Government, represented by the Home Secretary, Mr Chuter Ede, for the proper re-establishment of Alderney was shown in frequent visits from all three, both individually and occasionally collectively, during the second half of 1946 and early 1947.

The British Government having decided to write-off Guernsey's war debt of £2 million, the Bailiff proposed that Guernsey should, in return, accept responsibility for Alderney's financial position by underwriting her debts. Although this principal was accepted, and still exists today, in the intervening years between then and now, they have never actually been called on to do so. On one single occasion in the early days, Alderney had a budget deficit of £20,000 which it was authorized to meet from its own capital reserve fund which stood, at the time, at £52,000, and the island has always just managed to keep its head above water in this respect.

Jurat, Capt. Charles Richards, who had been appointed States' Treasurer and head of the Finance Committee, produced a budget for 1947, which expected to meet the necessary expenditure through the *Besoin Publique* and the *Impôt*. The Road Tax was not re-introduced. In the event, however, most of the 'rate-payers' managed to evade the tax of 2s. 6d. (12½p) per quarter of wheat rent, and only £350 was collected for the *Besoin*, while the *Impôt* in that year yielded £9,036, and the accounts overall showed a useful balance at the end of 1947.

In March 1947, as the communal farm experiment was not producing the expected results and most of the islanders wanted to be independent and work at their preferred occupations, and for their own rewards, Gen. Neame told the assembled islanders that the farm would be disbanded at the end of the year, and the British Government would hand the island back to the people on 31 December 1947, as had been agreed in the Resettlement Law 1945, after which they would be responsible for themselves. The Home Secretary asked for a report from the States by the end of July on what was still needed, which was duly discussed and submitted.

The result of this decision was for the Privy Council to hold an enquiry into the island's affairs and present status, and a searching questionnaire was sent out by Chuter Ede on 15 August 1947, which had to be completed and returned within eight days. Charles Batiste, the Greffier since 1921, was by now back at his post. The various members of the States dealt with the sections of this according to their own committee functions, ably assisted by Batiste, and returned the completed document. Many of the questions asked had concerned things which did not exist at all, such as a public health official or qualified schoolteachers, or were otherwise inadequately provided. The Commissioners of Crown Lands and the States each paid part of the small salaries of the appointed officials. The Judge received £350 per annum. The Procureur, who as Crown Prosecutor had to be qualified in both English and Norman Law, received £110 per annum, paid as £60 from the commissioners and £50 from the States. The Greffier received £25 per annum from the Crown, with an additional £24 for acting as registrar, along with fees for issuing birth and death cetificates, marriage licences, and making entries in the official records, and a 5 per cent commission on the stamp duties on documents from the States. The other paid officials received even smaller sums and the Sergeant had, in addition, a plot of land worth £3 a year in rent, but the positions of Sergeant and Sheriff were currently vacant in any case.

The salaries of the Harbour-Master, Crown Receiver and Gaoler were paid by the Commissioners of Crown Lands who also contributed to the salary of the vicar. The States paid the *Impôt* Receiver, the Inspector of Explosives, the Immigration Officer, School Attendance Officer and the Police Sergeant. The three ladies looking after the schoolchildren were paid £1 a week each. There was no external telephone system functioning, and the electricity was turned off at midnight.

The British Government responded helpfully to the deficiencies set out in the July report. The telephone service was re-instated by means of a somewhat unreliable radio link with Guernsey, despite its costing £1,000 per annum, and a rather inadequate island telephone system, adapted from the German set up, was first opened on 18 May 1949.

A number of new 'Ministry houses' were built by the Ministry of Works' mobile labour force, to replace those demolished by the Germans, with the owners only required to provide 15 per cent of the cost within six months of completion, if they had been the owners of the demolished property on 23 June 1940, and were once again permanently resident in Alderney by 25 September 1948. Other owners, not then resident but who gave notice by 1 June 1949 of their intention to occupy the building once it was completed, had to pay 15 per cent within six months, and the remaining 85 per cent of the rebuilding costs incurred on their behalf within a further twelve months. This last charge would be waived if the owner had been resident in the building concerned throughout that twelve month period. If they did not meet either of these requirements, they had to pay the full cost of repair or rebuilding within six months of completion of the work.

A headmaster, Mr Sladen, was sent for the school, while Maude Ollivier ran the junior school, and the States appointed the island's only doctor at that time, Dr Arkle, as medical officer of health. The Greffier's salary was raised to £350 as the islands first 'civil servant', and shortly after, on 20 October, the States took over the airport, the power installations, and subsequently the German water installations, the old French School, the dairy and the properties built or improved by both the German occupying forces, and by the British since the liberation. This was all carried out by compulsory purchase at pre-war values, plus some 5 per cent compensation. This was to be decided by independent arbitrators, the firm of estate agents, Lovell's in Guernsey, under the provisions of *The Acquisition of Improved Properties Law (Alderney), 1947* which had been drafted in March 1946 and received the Royal Assent on 8 August 1947. The purchase of the airport and power installations were actually paid for by the British Government although the money to be paid to the former owners of the land on which the airport was built was not distributed until the middle of 1949.

Unfortunately the States failed to take over some sections of paved roadways which the Germans had built across private land, and in 1991 there were still some anomalies in this respect causing small sections of the roadways to be left in a poor condition and disputes to arise over compulsory purchase and present valuations. This was finally corrected in 1992.

By 30 June 1947 the British Government had expended £174,000 on the rehabilitation work, and under the laws set out above much of this had to be repaid by 31 March 1953.

A Committee of Enquiry was set up by an order-in-council of King George VI, dated 3 July 1947, and was to consist of Lord Ammon, with the Home Secretary, the Rt. Hon. James Chuter Ede, MP, as chairman, and the Rt. Hon.

Osbert Peake, MP. Lord Ammon soon resigned, and on 8 August 1947 Viscount Stansgate, DSO was appointed to replace him.

The committee visited the island from 21 to 25 September 1947 and spent three days holding an enquiry at the militia arsenal and hearing evidence from States and *Douzaine* members about the pre-war conditions, employment, customs and laws in Alderney. At this time the population was 904, of whom 291 were on the electoral roll, and many of them attended the meetings. The island was still suffering considerably from the effects of the damage done during the occupation. The quarrying industry, the principal pre-war employer in the island, had not been restarted as most of its equipment had been either removed or badly damaged.

The committee did not think that the proposals put forward by the Alderney administration with regard to constitutional and economic matters were adequate to meet the needs, and as a result the Home Secretary paid another visit in January 1948.

One of the stumbling blocks appears to have been that it was not found possible at the time to produce documentary evidence of the status of the States as the governing body, or any laws prior to an order-in-council of 12 January 1916, with later orders of 28 November 1923 and 25 July 1934. All documents and records left in the island at the evacuation had vanished [1].

The committee was concerned that its recommendations, when made, should enable the island to become a viable community, with adequate standards of health, education and employment, and made suggestions for the expansion of the economy to meet these requirements. It seemed clear that the small population of Alderney could not service all its administrative needs, and a consultative committee was set up with Guernsey.

In November 1947, after the investigations of the Committee of Enquiry, Judge French resigned. The senior Jurat, Dan le Cocq, filled the vacant post of Judge for a short time, until Sir Frank Wiltshire MC, a friend of the Home Secretary, was called out of retirement in Birmingham to fill the post. The Home Secretary held another meeting in Alderney at the Militia Arsenal, on 17 January 1948, with Sir Frank Newsam KBE, CVO, MC, and Mr A.W. Peterson of the Home Office, the Lt. Governor and the Government Secretary Maj.-Gen. R.F. Colwill CBE, the new Judge, and the States' Controller, Mr P.M. Osmond, with the members of the States and the *Douzaine*.

---

[1] This is stated in the report of the committee, but seems strange since copies of many Alderney laws and constitutional matters were available in the Public Records Office, in correspondence between the Crown and Alderney's governors, and most orders-in-council, covering a period of at least 200 years, were available, in bound volumes, in Guernsey.

At this meeting, Mr Chuter Ede carefully explained to the assembled members what he thought they would find necessary in the way of income, to meet their needs and cover the expenses of the necessary staff to run education, health, airport and harbour, police services and the 'civil service', pensions, roads, and agricultural and food subsidies (rationing was still in force). The possibilities of their accepting close liaison with Guernsey over fiscal and tax matters were also discussed, while at the same time Mr Chuter Ede emphasized that they were a sovereign state, and were not compelled to accept his advice.

The new Judge held his first States' Meeting on 22 January 1948, and on 27 April a joint meeting was held between a committee from Alderney, consisting of the Judge, Jurats Richards and Kay-Mouat, *Douzenier* G. Jennings, People's Deputy W.P. Herivel and Mr H.G. Merson MBE, the Judge's personal assistant, and a similar group from Guernsey, consisting of the Bailiff who acted as chairman, Jurats Sir John Leale (president of the Guernsey Finance Committee), R.H. Johns, the States' financial secretary and States' assistant supervisor, and Mr E.T. Wheadon, deputy president of the Guernsey Board of Education.

The Alderney group stated that they aimed for the island to be wholly financially self-supporting, but would welcome administrative guidance and help from Guernsey for other services – police, education, health, pensions and social services, running the airfield, immigration, water, housing, sewerage and major roads.

They proposed to be self-governing in matters relating to public assistance, agriculture, minor roads, refuse collection and street cleaning, essential commodities, general sanitation and drainage, collection of motor tax, customs and excise duties, and dog and gun licence fees, erection of new houses and planning control, and the judicial administration.

In the discussion which followed it was noted that:

1. Alderney had one police sergeant who also acted as gaoler, a retired City of London policeman. If Guernsey took responsibility, it could replace the officer from time to time.

2. There were 100 children at the public school, where there was at present a vacancy for a headmaster, and 20 at the Convent, which had re-opened by then. The standards achieved did not at present permit Alderney children to take up scholarships in the Guernsey intermediate schools and colleges. It might later be possible to grade an Alderney school as a secondary modern, and pass children who achieved the necessary standards to Guernsey grammar or technical schools.

The same view as that on p. 72, in 1966, showing the runways

3. The airfield was now owned by Alderney, but the £4–5,000 per annum needed to maintain it was thought to be beyond Alderney's means. The Guernsey group very reluctantly agreed to recommend their States to accept responsibility for this.

4. They also agreed to recommend to the Guernsey States acceptance of responsibility for immigration, main roads and sewerage, social services and pensions, health services, and water supply – provided Alderney instituted a water rate charge, and certain administrative staff. It was thought that much of the cost of pensions might be met by a grant from the UK in respect of those Alderney residents who were, or had been, contributing to the UK National Insurance Fund during the war. The UK pension level was currently £75 p.a. Pensions had not hitherto been paid in Alderney, although legislation had been passed late in 1938 to allow payment of 10s. a week pension at age 65 but had not come into force.

Alderney agreed to institute, for the first time, income tax at the same level as Guernsey (2s. 6d. in the pound), and a revaluation of property, to assess rates for local services, at the average level of all the Guernsey parishes except St Peter Port.

The Judge also proposed reducing the size of the Alderney States to six or seven elected members presided over by the Judge, and to separate the judiciary completely, with three or four elected magistrates, but it was agreed to leave these subjects to the Privy Council Committee report. It was also agreed that Alderney should have two seats on the Guernsey States of Deliberation and four seats on the States of Election, that Guernsey should be responsible for the food subsidies, and that an advisory council be set up with three members from each island.

The minutes of the meeting were to be sent to the Home Office for approval and/or comment, there would be further discussion between the two sides, and the agreed matter should then be published in the *Billets* for both houses at approximately the same time.

The proposals were discussed in Alderney States on 16 July and in Guernsey on 21 July, and were approved in principle. The Alderney Investigation Committee met in August and September, and made its report on 18 October. The matters agreed were approved with certain stipulations regarding the Alderney water supplies, and with provisos that the future drafting of legislation in Alderney must be approved in Guernsey before being sent to the Privy Council, and that conditions of service, pay and pensions for the States' employees in Alderney should be the same as in Guernsey, as were to be general taxation levels, and rates, and the standards of education, health services, and old age pensions.

By agreement with the Home Office, most of the Crown Lands in Alderney were to be handed over to the States, except for the breakwater, which was thought to be too costly for Alderney to maintain. It was also agreed to supply a qualified land surveyor to re-establish the boundaries, and to repair the remaining war-damaged houses.

On 27 October these proposals met with general approval from the islanders at the People's Meeting, who voted in favour of the proposals by 138 votes to 6, and they were passed unanimously in the States of Alderney. It was debated in the Guernsey States on 5 November. The Alderney States acquiesced in this, *Alderney (Application of Legislation) Law, 1948*, on 1 December, which effectively passed to Guernsey the right to control the affairs of Alderney in many respects, 'As though those Islands were one'. Legislation also allowed for the setting up of the Land Commission to determine boundaries, and was embodied in *The Alderney Land and Property Law, 1949* which received the Royal Assent on 29 April 1949.

The cost of the Privy Council Committee investigations is recorded as £200, with a further £74 10s. for the printing of its report, which was not actually published until October 1949.

On 1 December the Alderney States also passed *The Government of Alderney Law, 1948*, which was registered in the Guernsey Greffe on 30 December 1948, and came into force on 1 January 1949.

While confirming all the laws and customs as they had previously existed in Alderney, except for those specifically dealt with in the new law, compared with the previous administrative and electoral procedures, drastic changes were about to take place. Proceedings were no longer to be conducted in French, save for the opening and closing reading of the Lord's Prayer in that language, and the *Billets* were to be published solely in English.

THE GOVERNMENT OF ALDERNEY LAW, 1948

Under the 1948 law all the previous offices and the States' system of government were abolished. Universal suffrage was decreed for all persons over the age of 20, who had been resident for more than a year on the 15 October each year, when the electoral roll would be updated. The administrative and judicial functions were separated, elections were to be held, as specified in the law, for the initial body of administrators as soon as an electoral roll had been prepared, and subsequently as set out in the law.

The head of the unpaid administration was to be a President, elected by the voters for a term of three years, after the initial two year term. This election to be held at least a week before the ordinary elections on each occasion. He would take precedence over all in Alderney, except the Lt. Governor or his representative, the Bailiff or his representative, and any member of the royal family actually representing the sovereign, and was to be supported by nine members of the States, each to serve for three years after the initial periods set out, after which one-third of the number would retire in rotation each year.

The judiciary was to consist in future of unpaid Jurats appointed by the Secretary of State, normally seven in number, one of whom would be designated as chairman. The real-property value qualification was removed. They would normally retire on reaching the age of 70, but this could be extended by a supplementary annual commission for the individual. Any three or more Jurats would constitute a court, the chairman to have an additional casting vote if necessary. They were empowered to deal with all civil cases, and with criminal cases where the punishment would not exceed a fine of £10, a month's imprisonment, or both, except for cases of treason, homicide, piracy, rape, arson, theft with violence, fraud or perjury, and cases where the punishment would be greater than the foregoing, all of which would be referred to the Royal Court in Guernsey. Most decisions of the Alderney Court could be appealed to the Royal Court. A paid Clerk of the Court, approved by the Secretary of State, and in the administrative sector a paid Clerk of the States (at first these were one and the same person, Mr Peter Radice), a surveyor or clerk of works, and a treasurer were appointed by him, and none of them could be dismissed without his approval.

The Clerk of the Court was to take over the functions of *Procureur du Roi*, Greffier, Sheriff, and Sergeant, but the court could appoint special constables to assist the members of the Guernsey Police on duty in Alderney. The *Douzaine* and the Poor Law board were disbanded.

Appointment as a Jurat, with certain safeguards, did not necessarily bar the individual from being either a States' Member or President. The oaths of office to be taken by Jurats, and by the President and States' Members were set out in *The Alderney (Forms of Oaths) Order, 1948.*

All of these paid and unpaid officials were to be ordinarily resident in Alderney, and are assumed to have vacated their offices if they ceased to be so, or were absent for more than two consecutive months. The States were to appoint a Finance Committee, and various other committees of which a quorum would be three, two of the States' Members were to represent Alderney in the Guernsey States of Deliberation, and four members to sit in the Guernsey States of Election.

Meetings of the States were to be open to the public, and before every States' Meeting, a People's Meeting of the electorate had to be held, with a member of the States as convenor. This meeting was for the purpose of discussing the various items included in the *Billet d'Etat* for that meeting, but the States' Members were not to be bound to vote in accordance with opinions expressed at the People's Meeting.

The various committees were to be reformed after each election, elect their own chairman from their number, and, except for the Finance Committee, were allowed to co-opt non-elected members provided they did not form a majority on the committee, and did not vote on anything involving taxes, rates, or expenditure. The States could also delegate various administrative functions to these committees, but the committees were not allowed to authorize employment of persons for longer than a week, or enter into any contract for expenditure unless that power had been delegated to the committee, and the States could not, in any case, enter into any contract, for goods or services, exceeding £100 without giving fourteen days notice in, 'a newspaper published in Guernsey and circulating in Alderney'.

This quite short, but far-reaching law became the basis for the Constitution of Alderney as it exists today, and, with only a few minor amendments, remained in force until the present, and not greatly different legislation, *The Government of Alderney Law, 1987*, came into force on 30 June 1987.

The first President of Alderney, Commander Sidney Herivel, was elected that same month (January 1949), and held the first meeting of the newly constituted States on 18 February. Commander Herivel held the post for twenty-one years until he resigned, only two weeks before his death. The last Judge, Sir Frank Wiltshire, had died just before the first meeting was held.

Minor amendments to the 1948 law were made in 1955 when the limit of the court's fines was raised to £25, the electoral-roll qualifications were changed slightly to exclude aliens, criminals and persons of unsound mind, and the qualification for seeking election to membership of the States or the office of President was increased from twelve months' to thirty-six months' residence. Of far greater importance was the inclusion by statute of the right of the people to address the States after giving due notice of the subject matter, at the sessions of Chief Pleas to be held, as formerly, in January and September, immediately preceeding the start of the States' Meeting. Other procedural amendments were included.

This statutory facility for electors in Alderney to address their parliament in session, directly, as a right, instead of by custom as was previously the case, is unique in both the Channel Islands and the British Isles. Unfortunately, perhaps through an oversight, there was nothing stated in the clause setting it up which required the States subsequently to act upon, or even to debate and consider, the subjects put forward by the people, an omission which makes this potentionally powerful, valuable, and unique right of the electors, virtually meaningless. In earlier times when it was merely a custom, from 'time-out-of-mind', to address the court presided over by the Judge, matters brought up by the people, both in common and of individual concern, had been discussed, and not infrequently acted upon. The origin of this Norman custom is thought to be with the Court of Pleas to which the people came to pay their rents, tithes and other dues, and at which time grievances were probably aired to the fee-farmer or his agent.

Further amendments were made in 1956, when States' employees were declared ineligible for membership of the States; in 1969 the maximum fine which could be imposed in Alderney was raised to £50; in 1970 election procedures were modified; in 1971 the number of elected States' Members was increased to 12; in 1975 the maximum fines were raised to £100 and the sentence which could be passed to two months, the age for eligibilty to vote was reduced to 18 years, the lower limit for contracts needing to be published was raised to £500, and Jurats were declared to be ineligible for the office of President, or as members of the States. In 1977 the voting procedures were again modified to allow postal votes by persons absent at the date of an election. In

1983 legislation was introduced to permit interest to be charged on unpaid debts to the court, and, finally, the whole 1948 law and amendments were replaced by the somewhat wider cover of the 1987 law.

Reference has already been made to the States taking over all former government property. The law to allow this was embodied in a statutory instrument, *The Alderney (Transfer of Property Etc.) Order, 1950*. By this act, in return for a payment of £10,000, the States acquired all of the quarries except Cachalière, although they were to own the foreshore and sea bed there, a considerable quantity of land, in addition to the above, amounting to about 140 acres, the remaining Crown-owned buildings, the Courthouse, gaol, etc., the inner harbour and the old harbour, the new pier and the attached German jetty, the lands formerly reserved round the coast for vraic-drying, the island of Burhou, and the sea bed within the territorial limits round the islands. The States also acquired the right to all Crown tithes and dues, wrecks (except for Crown vessels), and the *treizièmes (congé)* on property sales.

A reservation was made for the Crown to retain the breakwater, the mineral railway, the right to quarry stone free of charge from any of the quarries used for that purpose within the previous twelve months, to maintain the breakwater, the approaches to the breakwater, and land and stabling near York Hill quarry. They also retained the right to exercise troops on The Butes, Longis Common, and the foreshore 100 ft strips, and to extract water from springs at Valongis. Alderney, in future, had to appoint and pay the Harbour-Master, and pay the Crown portion of the vicar's stipend. This last item still figures in the annual accounts as a 'corn tithe' of £95, paid to the Church Commissioners.

THE LAND COMMISSIONER'S SURVEY AND PLANS

One of the stumbling blocks to the proper rehabilitation of the Alderney economy was the fact that, during the occupation, many of the boundary stones and markers had been removed. It was considered that it would be uneconomic to try and remove all the German defence works, and re-instate the land where they had been, and would be easier to bring other land into cultivation. In addition, to make the airport a viable entity meant encroaching further on the good agricultural land, and buying the ground from its owners. This could not be satisfactorily achieved until the ownership had been established.

The application of Norman inheritance laws over the centuries, and particularly since the division of the Common Lands in 1830, meant that real property had been divided among all children of a deceased person, with the eldest son receiving the largest share, and many of the resulting strips were only of a few perches. Sometimes members of the family had negotiated with each other to exchange, rent, or purchase adjacent strips, but there were many small holdings with scattered land. On 13 April 1949 the States passed *The Alderney Land and Property &c. Law, 1949* which received the Royal Assent on 29 April. This law set out, among other things, the establishment of an Alderney land register, under the control of the Clerk of the Court, acting as land registrar following the rebounding of the land by a land commissioner.

The commissioner was empowered to re-establish ownership as far as possible by open public enquiry, and to offer the opportunity for families to consolidate their holdings into more realistic plots by exchange. Where it proved impossible to determine ownership, the land was to be vested in the States, with a right of appeal by claimants within a specified time.

The final awards of the commissioners, and the plans drawn to delineate them, would form the basis of the Alderney land register. The laws of inheritance were amended to prevent the automatic splitting up of land in future, and a married women's property law was drafted in line with the Guernsey laws.

The work was commenced in 1949 by Capt. Otto Sigismund Doll who set up an office at 10 Victoria Street. He meticulously enquired into the claims of each and every land owner, and, with the assistance of 16-year-old Jimmy Cleal and an army surveyor's team including Frank Smith, gradually drew up maps in three separate sections to record his findings.

It was in some ways unfortunate that Capt. Doll had little or no knowledge of the French language, and as most of the individual holdings were known by the medieval field names of the enclosures, there was a certain amount of confusion between his phonetic spelling of what he was told, and existing maps and charts. Some of the first boundaries established were marked with elegantly cast concrete markers bearing the legend 'L S 1950', with an identification number in a shield above. The work proceeded very slowly, with sections 1 and 2 being finished in 1952 and 1955 respectively. Capt. Doll was unable to complete his work, and died in 1956. The survey was continued by Brig. W.M. Hayes, CBE, FRICS, who had a good knowledge of French, and who gathered together as many of the remaining title deeds still in existence as he could and had them all copied photographically, at the time an expensive and time-consuming activity. Unfortunately he retired in mid-1958, and died shortly after, and this work was never completed. His successor, Lt.-Col. S.H. Landfear, FRICS, was not allowed any further funds for this purpose. He carried on, and completed the register and a fourth map, in 1964.

Despite the length of time it had taken and the different personnel involved, the final maps are the definitive record of land ownership at that time, and have formed the basis of all transactions since. The remaining boundaries agreed by

Capt. Doll and his successors are marked with small square concrete posts bearing the impression E II and a number.

The land awards made as a result were embodied in numerical order of the plot numbers given them, in the Alderney land register, made up in registers of 100 properties by the Clerk of the Court, and the previous title deeds were then made redundant.

The people of Alderney were now once again confirmed in the possession of their land and property.

CHAPTER TWENTY-ONE

The Settlers

In about the middle of 1947 new settlers began to arrive in Alderney. One of the first to arrive was the eccentric author Tim White, who settled in a house in Connaught Square in the garden of which he later built a Greek theatre. Among his better known writings was the script for the musical *Camelot*, based on his book, *The Once and Future King*. These people, many of whom were retiring from British colonial administration, brought money and employment to the island, and houses were built to accommodate them, at first somewhat indiscriminately.

In 1948 some of the pre-war sporting activities were resumed. The Muratti Vase inter-island football games took place, with Alderney losing 3–0 to Guernsey. Alderney Week was restarted with Eileen Sykes (in 1992 vice-president of Alderney, and chairman of the Finance Committee) being elected as Miss Alderney 1948, and Pearl Venn being crowned in Guernsey as Miss Bailiwick.

The submarine HMS *Alderney* paid a visit, and tourists began to arrive. Trips to Burhou and France were run, and the cricket club was restarted, with Dr Ramsbotham, now back in the island, as scorer. Dr Ramsbotham joined Dr Kenneth Arkle who, up until then, had been the sole supplier of medical services to the island, as well as 'doubling up' as the vet.

The new laws for the Government of Alderney came into force on 1 January 1949 and, shortly after, Commander Sydney Herivel was elected first President of Alderney. His election was followed on 10 February by a general election for the nine seats on the new States' which were contested by thirty-two candidates.

The newly revived and repopulated island was honoured on 21 June by a visit from Princess Elizabeth and Prince Philip. The Princess, in responding to the loyal address by the president, referred to Alderney as, '. . . this small but precious jewel in my father's crown'.

With the Government of Alderney now set on a firm footing, more settlers began to arrive. After the end of the war, and with the beginnings of the breakup of the British Empire, many retiring service officers and former Colonial Servants, were looking for new homes. Apart from the peace and tranquillity of Alderney itself, the mild climate with little frost or snow, the freedom from many restrictions, the lower cost of homes, and lower taxation compared with the UK, made it an attractive proposition, despite its comparative isolation, difficulty of access, and the extra costs of transport for the essential commodities. The States also actively set out to attract 500 wealthy immigrants to the island.

The increase in population during this period can be seen from the census statistics. 1951 – 1,328; 1961 – 1,472; 1962 – 1,580; 1968 – 1,780.

Fifty Years On

To commemorate the fiftieth anniversary of the evacuation of Alderney, and the occupation of the Channel Islands, two events occurred in June 1990.

The first event was a visit to Alderney by the present mayor of Weymouth and the lady mayoress who took part in a ceremony at the harbour unveiling a plaque to commemorate the evacuation. More details of this event are given at the end of this chapter.

The second event was the making of a television programme for Channel TV. Records kept at the Alderney Society Museum were made available to the research team, and the author gave some assistance with the supply of photographs from his collection, and information from his own research.

The dedication ceremony of the fiftieth anniversary plaque

The mayor and mayoress of Weymouth with 100-year-old Mrs Phyllis Forsyth at the fiftieth anniversary celebrations

In the making of this programme, the director, Peter Batty, travelled to Germany where he found and interviewed a considerable number of survivors of the German troops who were present in the islands during the war. A number of them had spent time in Alderney, and I am indebted to Channel TV for permission to see the transcripts of many of the interviews, and to include some of their comments in this manuscript.

The comments of these members of the former occupying forces reinforces and confirms some things which have already been recorded in this book, although it is difficult to believe that in such a small island the troops were not aware of what was going on in the slave camps. Those who spent time in the other, populated, islands, in many cases appear to have met with a friendly reception from the inhabitants, and only a couple of those interviewed reported on a complete lack of response from the civilian population to their attempts at friendship.

Except for the first interview, the interviewees' anonymity has been preserved.

INTERVIEW 1

Dr Wilhelm Kasper, former German civil administrator in Guernsey, was asked what he thought would have happened if all the islands had been evacuated before the Germans arrived. He replied:

> Yes, we had an example of this in Alderney. The whole island had been evacuated before the Germans came, and there were Guernsey workers who cultivated the island with the help of an agricultural officer of the military government, but in the spring of 1943, he came to me and told me that the SS had come to the island and sent him away. He was so upset that he became a Trappist monk, who was not allowed to speak for the rest of his life. He, we, could not come to the island since that time, as it had been excluded from the military government.

There has long been a rumour circulating in Alderney that Hans Herzog, the civil affairs administrator, had become a Trappist monk, but his later contact

Germans in the deserted streets of Alderney, 1941–2

with the island when he sent letters, reports and the album of photographs, gave no indication of this, and one has tended to discount it. It would seem from this conversation that the person concerned might have been the agricultural officer, (K.V.R.) Pelz.

INTERVIEW 2

'Paul', evidently a senior Naval officer who had been sent to Alderney when it was first occupied, and had been stationed at Fort Albert, overlooking Norderney camp, gave many details of his time in the island. A summary of his interview follows.

When we arrived we found a lot of destroyed cars, empty houses and no people. About a week later Mr Osselton turned up. There was only him and his farmhand, he did not leave because he did not want to leave his cows.

He was about 50 years old, respectable, but sad because he had no cigarettes, so we traded for butter and fresh milk. He took me out fishing and knew where to find lobsters.

It was very boring for the soldiers so I formed study groups. I had several university graduates in various subjects, including a lecturer from Hanover University, and a lot of young soldiers who had just done their school exams and were pleased to go on studying: engineering, business studies, medical matters, etc. One landscape gardener suggested we should grow mushrooms in the old gun emplacements where they would always be damp and at a constant temperature. So I sent him home on leave to get some spores, and when he returned we got horse manure from the combat engineers, and started to grow them. We soon had enough to feed all of our 360 men once a week, it also gave them something to do.

The soldiers had to be drilled and made familiar with their weapons, the heavy guns and cannons, but you can't do that 24 hours a day, most of them had never been in combat, and there was nothing much of a front line here. We could go for walks but there were maybe two dozen trees and about 100 bushes and the rest was fields and rocks. There was a problem with an enormous number of rats in Fort Albert. At first we tried to catch them and kill them with our dogs, but that didn't work. Our cook, who had worked on board a steamer, had a cage made and put two in without food or water. They soon began to gnaw each other and their screams drove the others away. You could see a trail of 5–600 rats making for the sea like lemmings, and we didn't have much trouble after that.

German soldiers manning a heavy gun on a revolving platform, Batterie Blücher, 1941

Our routine was: reveille at 6 a.m.; 7 a.m. – inspection; 8 a.m. – start work. The active troops manned the heavy guns, and I had 200 recruits to instruct. We also had sports and competitions. We only had to fight once, and then we fired on our own German boats. When the *Prince Eugen* broke out at the end of 1941, the *Luftwaffe* gave me a plan of grid squares, and our range-finders tracked a group of ships moving towards us in line abreast. We fired on them, and after the second shot got a recognition signal. Two hours later we were told that a group of minesweepers would be clearing a passage for the big ships! Years after the war I found that my sister-in-law's husband had been in command of the minesweepers!

Asked about the *Todt Organisation* camps, he said:

First I only knew they were volunteer labourers from the east. Some time later I saw they were living under the most miserable conditions, and there was a guard, a black negro who beat them mercilessly. I had the leader of the camp brought to me and told him that if it happened again I would shoot the negro. I think that stopped it, but many labourers died through malnutrition, weakness and exhaustion. I never went into the camp, but only watched from above. Much later it was found that a lot of their food had been sent home. Those responsible were removed. The sick were put on a boat to be transported to the mainland, but a great storm arose and the boat with the Ukrainians broke loose. My friend Ingsandt tried to tow them with his *Voorpost* boat, but hadn't enough steam, and ran aground. His boat was still there long after. I had no contact with the OT, only the commander of the Pioneer Unit from whom I borrowed some corporals to drill my men. I know there was another camp full of Jehovah's Witnesses, it was a sort of concentration camp but we kept well out of the way.

INTERVIEW 3

In Alderney everything was empty, the houses were all deserted and we were divided into three watches, one at the harbour, one at the fort [almost certainly Fort Tourgis], and one other. We were only allowed to send home 50 gm, so as far as I was concerned that was stockings for the women

Fetching lunch up from Fort Tourgis, August 1941 (see p. 96)

and nothing else. The airforce had already been there, and they say they had taken away most of it, so the island was a sorry sight. Once I had the experience of an English bomber coming over. It dropped four bombs, one fell in the harbour, one on the beach, and the other two on the other side of the island. With my soldiers I had to go on harbour watch, but there was nothing else to do except go for walks.

This soldier was later transferred to Sark, and 'found it was like being at home'. Later still he was sent to Jersey.

INTERVIEW 4

Alderney was quiet because nobody was there. I heard there was one civilian but he must have been on the other side of the island and I never saw him. Nothing was destroyed, the houses were suddenly deserted, but the airforce had been through them before us. I was in Alderney about three months, and all there was to do was to walk along the beach, and look for a farm.

Capt. Jacobeit, a former pharmacist from Stettin, November 1941

INTERVIEW 5

This artilleryman, who had been in England as a schoolboy, came to Alderney in a boat from Granville, shortly after the fall of France, but was soon sent to Jersey, which he enjoyed.

It was a funny feeling because there were no inhabitants, only this battery Alsace with the crew, and two or four companies of infantry. Conditions were not good, there was this brand new battery in very old casemates and a lot of rats running about. We lived in the old casemates. There was a bit of a problem with alcohol, because there was nothing to do except sit in the damp casemates and drink.

INTERVIEW 6

The subject of this interview was one of the German political prisoner survivors from Sylt camp, to which he was transferred from Sachsenhausen in 1943, having first been imprisoned for 'subversive activities' against Hitler in 1934.

We were sent to Dusseldorf to look for unexploded bombs, it was a suicide squad, 112 died. They made the survivors up to 1,000, with men from Buchenwald, and we went to Alderney. Here the camp was only partly finished – there were four or five huts. We lay out in the open until we had built the barracks, then we worked on bunkers, fortifications, roads and cable-laying. We were under the supervision of the SS day and night, and were not allowed to leave the camp at all [on their own].

Conditions were terrible, we were supposed to get the same rations as the armed forces because we were manual workers, but we didn't get them, because the SS had double helpings, and sold the food on the black market. The camp commandant, List, went on leave and was checked by the military police; he had whole chests full of sugar, lard, dripping, bacon, etc.

We got up at 5 a.m., cleaned the barracks and had breakfast, and had roll-call. We went to work at 6 or 7 o'clock depending on the time of year. Watery soup for lunch, a bit of turnip or cabbage in it, where we were working. At 6 p.m. we finished work, and were checked again, that always took hours. Everyone got a piece of bread – 1,000 gm, and 10 gm margarine between six people. Sometimes a slice of sausage or a bit of cheese. To drink, something called coffee. We had a lot of beatings and mistreatment. One man moved a few steps from his place of work and got twenty-five lashes. We had a large number of Russians there and they called it 'twenty-five hollies'. A number of the inmates were hanged, they called it suicide. *Obersturmführer* Klebeck gave the orders and the prisoners Fahrenbacher and von Traurer did it and got a reward. Many died of malnutrition, and about thirty got TB. They were 'shot, trying to escape', a hole was cut in the wire, they were forced to go through it and shot outside. From 1,000, when we left, there were only about 650 of us. About 80 per cent were foreigners, mostly Russian. Of the Germans, 140–50 were so-called 'professional criminals' with green stripes and green initials. There were only about 50–60 political prisoners, their files were marked 'RU' – Return Undesirable.

We had no contact at all with other people, and after the Allies landed in Normandy orders were issued by Lt.-Col. Schwalm to our camp commandant, that if the island were attacked all prisoners were to be placed under armed supervision, and that no-one was to fall into the enemy's hands alive. In general we had had a good relationship with the *Wehrmacht*, they often slipped us food if they were able, they stood on guard because they had to.

After the war the British authorities didn't bother much about the crimes committed on Alderney, they would have preferred it if no-one knew of the camp, and said the crimes were not committed against Britons. After the war I tried to get a memorial erected on the site of the camp, and involved Mr Pantcheff, but the authorities would not permit it. Criminal proceedings were started against Klebeck and Hegelhohe after the war, and they imprisoned Hegelhohe then, but when Germany took over the political power in 1957 or 1958, they were all given amnesty. List lived near Hamburg and was interrogated by the DPP in about 1970, but said he didn't know Alderney and it must be a case of mistaken identity. They let him go.

INTERVIEW 7

I was only in Alderney at the base for four weeks. We went for walks through the harbour and the town. There were a few civilians here and there, and we saw the concentration camp prisoners disembarked at the harbour. Otherwise we were on day or night guard duty.

INTERVIEW 8

I think Alderney was very stupid, there was no cinema, no dancing and our soldiers were very young. We had our canteen and our duties and that's all. We were at Fort Albert at first and there were lots of rats, but the cook got rid of them [see above]. After a week Mr Osselton came to us and said he

German troops and one of the goats left behind, 1942

was the last inhabitant of Alderney but had no cigarettes, so we swapped for butter and milk. He showed us where to find lobsters, and big oysters which you must pull up quickly and eat like *wiener schnitzel* [ormers]. He stayed because of his cows, and was a good friend. When I went away in July 1943 he said he would like to come with me, but I was going in a submarine, and he said he wouldn't like that.

We repaired some of the houses for our soldiers, and then tried to fix some of the cars. We managed to get a Morris Commercial bus going from the bits of three or four cars, and could get to the harbour to collect our food. People didn't enjoy their time in Alderney, it was just duty.

The final chapter in this story occurred on Sunday 24 June 1990, fifty years from that fateful Sunday when almost the whole population of Alderney left their homes and possessions, and sailed for Weymouth.

Many of the survivors of those who returned to Alderney in 1945–6 after the war attended a ceremony at the harbour. A total of about 160 people, including Mrs Phyllis Forsyth, who was to be 100 years old on 10 July, had originally returned.

Mrs Forsyth had taught in the Alderney school before the war, served on the Alderney Relief Committee throughout the period of exile, and was one of the first group to return to the island when hostilities ceased.

The present mayor and mayoress of Weymouth, the town where the refugees had landed in 1940, had come to unveil a plaque commemorating the event, at the harbour from which they sailed. A simple commemorative service was held jointly by the new vicar, Revd Stephen Ingham, the Catholic priest, Father Henry Bradley, the Methodist minister, Mr Geoffrey Blackmore, and the Salvation Army leader, Lt. Jim Smith.

At the same time the mayor and mayoress presented the island with a decorated plate (see p. vi) made in their local pottery commemorating the arrival of the evacuees in Weymouth. This may now be seen in the Alderney museum.

This solemn occasion was supported by a large number of today's islanders, out of respect for the courage and fortitude shown by the older generation who had either to abandon their homeland, or stay and face oppression, and who had departed into the unknown on Sunday 23 June 1940.

The commemorative plaque in the harbour wall

German Names for Alderney Places

Naturally enough the English or French names for Alderney's streets, bays and features did not suit the German powers, and most of them were given new names. In many cases, of course, a simple translation of the previous name was sufficient, but a few do not relate quite so obviously.

Most of the more important of those to which I have found reference are listed below with their earlier local designations; if different again, the present-day name is given in brackets.

GERMAN NAME	PREVIOUS NAME
Forts	
Josephsburg	Fort Grosnez
Bergfeste	Mount Hale Battery
Schirrhof	The Arsenal
Rosenfeste	Roselle Battery
Albert Burg	Fort Albert
Einsiedler Schloss	Château à L'Etoc
Strandefeste	Fort Corblets
Hummefeste	Fort Hommeaux Florains
Dachfeste	Fort Quesnard
Ostefeste	Fort Houmet Herbè
Eilandefeste	Fort Raz
Piratenschloss	The Nunnery
Burg Essex	Fort Essex
Steinfeste or Steinburg	Fort Clonque
Türkenburg or Tuerkenburg	Fort Tourgis

Salzfeste   Fort Platte Saline
Dohlenfeste   Fort Doyle

Bays
Hafen-bucht   Braye
Norder Bucht   Saye
Bade Bucht   Corblets
Fischer Bucht   Vau Tremblièrs
Khatzen Bucht   Cats
Lange Bucht   Longis
Schüler Bucht   La Tchue
Telegrafenbucht   Telegraph
Drei-Berge-Bucht   Trois Vaux Bay
Hanna-bucht   Hannaine
Felsen Bucht   Clonque
Salz-bucht   Saline
Krabbenbucht   Crabby

Headlands and Rocks etc.
Bieberkopf   Bibette Head
Hühnerfeste   Brinchetais Reef
Kaninchenbucht   Les Becquets
Südhafen   Cachalière
Schwarzer Felsen   Noire Rogue
Austernfelsen   Coque Lihou
Zwillingfelsen   Fourquie
Putenfelsen   Les Noir Putes
Gutenburg   Tête de Judemarre
Drei Berge Felsen   Les Étacs (Garden Rocks)

Quarries
Steinbruch   Mannez
Vorderbruch   Berry's
Grosser Bruch   Battery Quarry

Places and Building
Borkhumhäuser   Essex House (The Devereux Hotel)
Grave Häuser   Whitegates
Hafen   The Harbour
Hafenstadt   Braye Village

Haus Keller	Longis Villas
Horningsheim	Simon's Place
Marienplatz	Marais Square
Millionärshof	Quatre-Vents
Mole	The Breakwater
Müllerhof	Watermill Farm
Neustadt	Newtown
Plattenberg	The Butes
Rosenhof	Rose Farm
Rotes Haus	Coastguards
Soldatenheim	The Convent (The Island Hall)
Soldatenkino	The Rink (now demolished)
Tafelberg	Le Rond But

Bibliography

(Place of publication given only if outside London.)

Alderney Society, *Bulletin*. 1966–89.

——, *An Alderney Scrapbook*. Alderney, 1972.

Alvarez, J.E., *German Occupation of the Channel Islands*. (unpub. thesis, Michigan University, 1985).

Antill, J.K., *A Bibliography of the German Occupation of Jersey and other Channel Islands*. Jersey Greffe, 1975.

Aufsess, Baron von und zu, *Occupation Diary*. Chichester, Phillimore, 1985.

Bonnard, B., *Island of Dread in the Channel*. Stroud, Alan Sutton Publishing, 1991.

——, *Alderney in Old Photographs*. Stroud, Alan Sutton Publishing, 1991.

Channel Island Occupation Society. *Channel Islands Occupation Review*. Annual publications, CIOS, 1972–92.

——, *Verstärkung der Kanalinseln*. CIOS Archives Book, No. 3, 1941.

——, *Channel Island Merchant Shipping 1940–1945*. CIOS Archives Book, No 5.

Cooper, Bryan, *The Battle of the Torpedo Boats*. 1972.

Cruikshank, C., *The German Occupation of the Channel Islands*. Guernsey, The Guernsey Press, 1975.

Dalmau, J., *Slave Worker in the Channel Islands*. Guernsey, Private pub., 1954.

Ginns, M., *A Guide to Alderney's German Fortifications*. Alderney, The Alderney Society, 1981.

Hynes C.A., and Partridge, C., *A Guide to the Fortifications of Alderney 3. German*. Alderney, The Alderney Society, 1980.

King, P., *The Channel Islands War 1940–1945*. Robert Hale, 1991.

Kondakov, G.I., Personal Communications.

Mayne, R., *Channel Islands Occupied*. Norwich, Jarrold & Sons, 1985.

Nebel, G., '*Bei den Nordlichen Hesperiden', Tagebuch aus dem Jahre 1942*. 1948.

Pantcheff, T.X.H., *Alderney, Fortress Island*. Chichester, Phillimore, 1981.

Partridge, C.,   *Hitler's Atlantic Wall*. DI Publications, 1976.

Ramsey, W.G., *The War in the Channel Islands. Then & Now*. After the Battle Publications, 1981.

St John Packe, M., and Dreyfus, M., *The Alderney Story 1939/49*. Alderney, The Alderney Society, 1971.

Saunders, H. St.G., *The Green Beret*. 1949.
Steckoll, S.H., *The Alderney Death Camp*. Granada, 1982.
Toms, Carel, *Hitler's Fortress Islands*. New English Library, 1967.
Trevor-Roper, H.R., *Hitler's War Directories*. 1964.

Index